McVanBuck

Guns, Grizzlies, And Scares

Peter N. Mast

McVanBuck Publishing Edition

© 2022 September First Printing

Copyright by Peter N. Mast

ISBN: 978-1-7770530-5-5

Illustrations by Peter N. Mast

Find more information online at
www.mcvanbuck.com

Email mcvanbuck@gmail.com

Saskatchewan, Canada

Peter N. Mast
Box 1040
Kinistino, SK
Canada
S0J 1H0

Special Thanks!

To all the many McVanBuck readers out there –
there's too many to count – thank you for all of your
kind words, telling me of how you truly laughed and
enjoyed the stories. I had just as much fun hearing
of your joy of you reading the stories to your
families, as I had in writing them.

Thank you to Joy Mast, my wife, who has done
most of the excellent, fine-tune English editing for
the McVanBuck book series.

Thank you to Heather Mast, who spent many
hours helping us edit the first book called,
McVanBuck Call of the Lighter. The fact that you
were only a teenager and you did this all while
working a job, is truly astonishing. I am, indeed,
very proud of you. No words can tell you how much
this meant to me. This work is now cemented in the
land of forever, for great books never die, and
neither will your works. I will see you soon at the
lake with your beautiful wide smile and in your
green Coleman canoe to catch the monster
Northern Pike that keeps eluding us.

Thank you to Martin Mast for recording and
producing, *McVanBuck Call of the Lighter* Audio
Book. Your many great professional, different
character voices brought the book to life. You are a
gifted voice artist indeed, and are an amazing
person. My trigger finger is itching to shoot some
clay pigeons Saturday afternoon, we will see you
then.

And to all my children who do a big part of the
proof reading: Quinton, KJ, Julie, Monica and
Crystal Mast. I am so blessed to have so many
smart and hard-working people, so close to home. I
have had many great laughs, writing these books
with you all. There have been many great lines in

these stories that have come out of our conversations, as I have recounted these stories to you all, over the years. Your mom and I are very blessed to have you as our children.

Thank you so much to my Canadian and American relatives who purchased my first book *McVanBuck Call of the Lighter.* You then actually read the book, and said you loved it! Wow!

Like it is said in the book business, "you don't truly know who likes your writing style, until they buy it and then you hear that they loved it." Now I know who truly likes my humour writing. Your encouragement warmed my heart, telling me you truly loved the McVanBuck stories and characters. Some of you even compared my writings to those of the great and famous outdoors humour writer, Patrick F. McManus. I am truly honored and humbled. I hope you enjoy these new stories as much as you did the stories in the first book.

Disclaimer

Some of you have said that the cartoon-looking characters I drew resemble some people I know. My answer is yes, I do admit they do look a little similar. There was no ill intent meant by it, but only the highest of honor.

These stories are based on true events, but some of the names of the characters, places, times, things they said or did not say, and things they did or did not do - have been modified a little for obvious safety reasons.

Unfortunately, I could not be 100 percent accurate all of the time; but like the saying goes, "the pen is mightier than the bullet... but a bullet makes for a very short writing career."

My reasons for writing these stories were simple: to tell the greatest Canadian adventure stories there are to be told; and to bring a little laughter and sunshine into your day.

Contents

Introduction

The McVanBuck family are up to it again, with their old unbreakable mindset of "do it first – it's faster than thinking."

Some of you may find some wisdom to be had in this second book of the McVanBuck series, if you can stop laughing long enough to see it.

As for the outdoors men and the hunter, you will learn to be lucky in the backwoods to avoid being accidentally shot and luckier still, by voiding being mauled by the hands of an enraged grizzly bear. What to do when the enraged bear gets so close that you can smell their breath? You drop your rifle from your shoulder to your hip, and then like a skilled gun slinger, you try a cocky hipshot to stop the bear from mauling you to death. But, of course, you have never practised the hipshot, neither have you ever attempted it before...

Chapter 1.

^

Hunting Gophers
&
Pompoms Balls

My introduction to hunting and the intense adrenaline rush it can bring on a fellow in unsuspecting ways, began about thirty years ago. We McVanBucks, who lived in Alberta, made plenty of days for hunting. Starting in the springtime, there were the prairie gophers that needed to be hunted. This then led into the fall, where every big game animal that could be hunted (like moose, deer, and bear) was shot and then eaten.

The prairie gophers were not normally eaten, for they were classified as nuisance vermin. But some of my kin have been known to eat them, from time to time. This mostly occurred when an individual took the quote, "What you shoot, is what you eat," out of context and to the extremes of a hard-core hunt.

The extreme hard-core hunter would have small game animals on their menu, like gophers, magpies, and the occasional house mouse, from the mouse trap in the corner.

As for the extreme, hard-core trapper, they would not just eat the small game they caught, but they would also skin them out. They would then, on occasion, fiddle excessively with the pelts, while entertaining young children with their mouse finger puppets.

My Uncle Casper would say, "Look, children! I've got a puppet on each of my fingers. One to come after each of you, squeak-ety-squeak, squeak-ety-squeak, the mice are coming for you, hahaha!"

Uncle Casper would then try to dance his homemade mouse puppets on the top of the children's heads.

The children would then flee in terror, screaming, "Ahhhh... Mommy, Mommy!" Crawling on his hands and knees after the children, he'd make his mice look like they were trying to run up the bottom cuffs of the boys' trousers.

Now, my Uncle Casper was a hard-core trapper and a creative skilled craftsman, for he made some fine leather-fur crazy-quilts. About fifty percent of each quilt was made out of gopher hides, and the rest was made up from the hides of pack rats, mice, and chipmunks.

One Christmas while over at my grandparents' house, Uncle Casper enthusiastically asked my dad, "So, Elvis, what do you think of your Christmas present? Can you believe that I made it myself? Sure had a hard time getting that pack-rat scent off my hands, but just look at what I made! The pack rats I had to go out of province to get; since it's a specialty market and all."

"Why, that's a mighty fine lookin'…a… hmm… you couldn't get the pack-rat musk smell out of the blanket though, eh? It'll keep the dog mighty warm this winter, I'm athinkin'," my dad responded.

"What do you mean keep the dog warm?" Uncle Casper croaked out. "It's not for your dog!? What is he? Royalty?"

My dad rethought his answer carefully. "Come to think of it, maybe one of my kids could use it."

Uncle Casper grumbled, "Cripes, you sure are insensitive. I made that for your bed and the missus. If you wait a minute, 'til your five kids unwrap their Christmas presents, you'll see I've made each one of them a beautiful quilt for their bed also, just like this one!"

Prairie gopher hunting was a yearly task to control the vast multitudes of gopher holes on the pastures of Canadian ranch land. It also helped to keep the Black Plague at bay that these gophers, unfortunately, could carry. This yearly hunt consisted of my two younger brothers (Nedge and Calvin) and I heading out with our .22 caliber rifles along with our thirty-round banana clips and hollow-point shells to conquer this menace, and to bring complete eradication to these ground-burying squirrels on our parents' farm.

Now, I know I said "eradication," but this word can be overridden by the word "rationed" when employed along with the words "yearly goals". Plainly speaking, we liked hunting gophers, some of us even LOVED hunting gophers. The hard-core lovers of this depopulation sport can also be referred to as "trigger happy" by some. You can spot this "trigger happy" disease, by the size of the large grin on the hunter's face as they purchase the case of a thousand shells at the gun store, instead of the normal small box of fifty. And the well-established, thick callus on their trigger finger is also a dead giveaway.

We needed to use a great deal of self-control to not completely wipe out the gopher colony, but only bring it down to a manageable level and slow the plague of these breeding machines and their love affair with digging. Do they really need to have thirty back doors in their home to take the bag of trash out to the curb on Thursdays? Probably not...

Sometimes, we along with the neighbor boy Rodney, who was about eighteen and was several years older than us, would spend a couple of hours thinning down the gopher population in the back pasture. We'd shoot at the biggest gophers on this side of the Canadian border.

Rodney was a big teen boy, and was built like a man with his German ancestry. He spoke perfect English, even though the rest of his family carried strong German accents.

It was a cool, early-spring, Saturday afternoon, and Rodney had come over to go gopher hunting with me. Nedge had left for the weekend, and Calvin was preoccupied, helping Dad to mount a new scope on Calvin's new bolt-action Remington .22 rifle that had a removable, ten-bullet magazine clip.

Rodney and I had healthy trigger fingers, that were itching for some game to hunt after a long winter. With an ample supply of targets awaiting us, who were just waking up from their winter hibernation nap, we headed out to the pasture.

I said, "Okay, Rodney, I'll let you start the slaughter first. Once you've got your thirty shots off, then I'll give it a go. Let's go and head over to the far end of the high hills, to Massacre Mound. I saw a good whack of them gophers over there yesterday."

"Sounds solid to me," came Rodney's reply, as he finished loading his magazine clip with bullets, and we started walking in that direction with our guns resting in our arms.

Now the main gopher colony was located among the dirt mounds that had been created when the dugout for water was built. This gave the gophers large mounds of dirt to dig in that stood about twelve feet in height and ran the length of the 100-foot long dugout. Grass had been planted; and over the years, the dirt piles had become hilly pasture land.

As the gophers popped up their heads, out of one of their thirty back doors, we were busily plunking gopher after gopher, when I noticed one of the gophers running along the top edge of the mound.

Excitedly, I said to Rodney, "Over there! Do you see over there's a big fat gopher trying to run away? Quick!.. get it! My clip just ran dry."

Rodney had just finished reloading thirty bullets into his clip.

In a flash, ten rounds of shells were fired-off from his semi-automatic long-rifle gun in quick succession, *Bang, Bang, Bang, Bang, Bang, Bang, Bang, Bang, Bang, Bang,* at this running gopher before it disappeared behind the mound of dirt.

Then turning to me with a confused look on his face, he asked, "Are you sure that was a gopher? It looked... odd."

As a curl of smoke rose out of his gun barrel, I reassured him, "You bet it is, and a big gopher at that!"

Then a moment later, the gopher was back, but now only twenty feet away from where he had first disappeared. He was again running along the top edge of the dirt bank.

I said, "There he goes again!"

There was the sweet-sounding flurry of fifteen shells passing through the barrel of Rodney's semi-automatic gun, *Bang, Bang, Bang, Bang, Bang, Bang, Bang, Bang, Bang, Bang, Bang, Bang, Bang, Bang, Bang,* before the gopher disappeared behind the mound once again, as it worked its way along the edge, getting closer to us.

"Man!" I said, "He's a sneaky one."

"No fear, I'll get'im! I'll be ready... if he shows up again, I'll get'im," replied Rodney, as he tweaked the scope knob of his rifle with his fingertips and moved onto his belly, into a sniping position.

Then the gopher appeared again, and the last five shells in Rodney's clip rattled off. *Bang, Bang, Bang, Bang, Bang*

Rodney declared, "I swear, I hit that thing at least twenty times."

This was believable, for he was a good shot.

And it had looked to me, as the gopher ran along the top of the mound, like it was being hit.

"This is one tough gopher... he must've got a thick layer of armour on. I thought I saw a piece of him flyin' apart," I said with a chuckle.

"Perhaps," suggested Rodney, "the adjustment on my rifle's scope has come loose."

"Yeah," I said, "Maybe there's a loose screw on it."

As we examined the gun in confusion as to its inability to pick off that big gopher, a voice cried out from behind the large mound of dirt, "QUIT THE SHOOTIN, YOU FOOLS'! WE'S THE PEOPLE ARE OVER HERE."

This voice sounded just like the voice of my dad - and not the terrified chirping of a ground squirrel.

Then we saw a winter hat, rising up from behind the large mound of dirt. Dad had placed his toque on the end of his rifle barrel and was now using it as his make-shift flag of surrender, as he waved it from side to side.

He bellowed, "QUIT THE SHOOTIN'! WE'S ARE A-COMING OUT."

Rodney and I stared at each other in disbelief, and I felt a terrible case of indigestion enter into my stomach, making me feel sick.

When I glanced over at Rodney, I saw that all of the colour was draining out of his face.

Starting from the top of his forehead, the colour drained away, passing through his once happy grin, and it left out through the bottom of his chin.

When Dad and Calvin emerged from behind the mound of dirt, along the left side – out in front of us, I noticed right away that something was definitely wrong with the red and white winter toque that was now put back on the top of Dad's head.

The pom-pom ball was in tatters. In fact, there was only a strand or two of wool yarn still intact, of what once was a full pom-pom that had been about the size of a baseball, which had been sewn onto the top of his winter toque. We were no Wild Buffalo Bill Hickok, shooting a man's pom-pom ball off the top of his head for some thrilling entertainment, to show off our shooting skills.

"I's could hear the zingin' sounds 'round the top of my head," Dad began between his frightened breaths, his extremities visibly quivering. "I thought thems were a hoard of bees, at the first. Then me and Calvin heards it happenin' again! I know it was no bees! Had me's thinkin' maybe something's wrong with me ears, but Calvin's heard it, too. After the third blast, it hit me - as pieces of my toque started fallin' down in front of my eyes, into my hands! Then I remembered, ya' boys were over here, somewhere's, shooting them gophers. We hit the deck then, ...started yellin' from our bellies at ya fellows to quit the shootin'!"

Then it hit me why the gopher had looked so weird. I had thought, at the time, that my eyes were playing tricks on me. The gopher wasn't wearing a bright, red and white life-jacket, for it wasn't even a gopher; and it was no mere illusion of the sun-rays hitting a scampering gopher - it was the pom-pom ball on the top of Dad's toque!

After that close affair with near-death passing over his head; my dad, Elvis, never again, owned a toque with a pom-pom ball on the top of it. And if a new toque came into his possession with the customary pom-pom ball attached to it, the ball would immediately disappear. Dad would quickly pop the yarn ball off his new winter hat with a quick, sharp jerk while giving me a chilling, uncomfortable glare without saying a word.

Now, I have done a lot of foolish, unintentional things in my lifetime, but this was about the dumbest of them all.

Unfortunate Close-Call Event

This event is based on a true story that I would have preferred to never have happened to me in the first place. I still blush with shame 30 years later. My hope in sharing this experience with you is that some can learn by it and not fall into a McVanBuck moment when using a fire-arm while high on adrenaline and triger-finger fever. Fire-arms are an excellent tool for hunting, shooting clay-pigeons, target practicing at the range, and for work in the military and the police. A fire-arm, also, defended my very life from a grizzly bear attack. Yet, a fire-arm should never be pointed in the direction of a human being, except by the military and the police. In that case, you can gun people down and even get paid to do it.

As for this story, Elvis and Calvin could have avoided this close call simply by calling out to make their presence known before they entered the known shooting area. And secondly, they could have come in from a angle that would have been visible to the shooters.

As for the hunters and sportsmen out there, please take fire-arm safety seriously, so that we all might arrive home alive, to hunt another day.

Chapter 2.

^ ^

Firefighting
&
Geyser Riding

Wind conditions shouldn't be underestimated when you've got a fire that's burning out of control, especially when it's on dry grassland. Also, the fire shouldn't be underestimated if it's anywhere near to a person who has a last name of McVanBuck – unless you are in need of an expert opinion on how to fight a wall of fire with an even larger wall of fire, while using the wind as leverage.

This expert McVanBuck knowledge will definitely tell you if the particular fire that you are inquiring about is, in fact, out of control. Once you have gained this information - that the fire is, indeed, out of control - it is best not to ask a McVanBuck any further questions of how to put your fire out, unless you are in need of an unique extinguishing method. These McVanBuck methods are, indeed, effective in getting the job done, but are of the less-than-popular, fire-extinguishing methods.

One such fire occurred on a hot fall day, when I was about thirteen years old. This wild prairie fire was quietly brewing and was only a breath away from erupting. Grandpa McVanBuck was baling small square straw bales out in the fields at the time, driving his old Case tractor.

Back at the farmhouse, Mom called to me, "Peter, do you want to come out to the field with me? I need to bring Grandpa some lunch."

The lunch for Grandpa consisted of some leftover fried chicken, mashed potatoes and gravy, with a banana on the side, and a glass-quart jar of iced tea to drink.

I replied excitedly, "You bet, Mom! Maybe Grandpa will need me to drive the tractor, while he eats his lunch."

Mom responded, "I do not think so...

perhaps when you get a little older and a little more mature."

I said emphatically, with irritation in my voice, "But, Mom, I am mature."

"Well, Peter, you know what I mean. We don't have time today to fix stuff after you break it," she continued, as we headed out the front door.

I did not know for certain what broken stuff, she was specifically talking about. If it was the time I ran the car into the tree, when she had left me in the car while it was still running and I had shifted the car into gear... well, that had happened back a long time ago – back when I was only four years old. And I was real sorry over it afterwards. And if it was when I smashed into the cow fence with the pickup truck, that was... well again, at least a week ago. And I was real sorry about that as well.

We got into the car, and Mom drove out into the field to give Grandpa his noontime dinner. As we approached the field, we could see some white billowing smoke coming from the far end of the field, where the barley straw was currently in the process of being baled.

Now, this was not highly alarming to us, at the time, for there had been a brush pile burning back there from the previous winter. The brush pile had continued smouldering through the following spring and summer, and now, was still smouldering into the current fall harvest.

As we drove across the field, we could see Grandpa on the tractor cutting across all the swaths of straw that had not even been baled yet. The tractor was blowing black smoke out of its diesel engine, as it raced through the field in high gear.

Then Mom and I watched, as he began to also indiscriminately run over the straw bales that he had just baled that very same day. The tractor was still pulling the baler behind itself. This appeared to our eyes, like an act of madness.

Out loud, Mom asked the single question that was in her mind, as she drove the car closer in the direction of the speeding tractor that was now heading towards us.

"What is he doing?"

Excitedly, I exclaimed, "Grandpa's driving over the new bales, Mom!"

She responded, "Well, I can see that... but why? There must be something wrong with Grandpa!"

I didn't think Grandpa had lost his mind, for he was a man who was not in the habit of losing his mind when things went wrong.

I thought to myself, *Perhaps he was like a man who had just baled his last bale and had decided to just quit his job on the spur of the moment. But what fun would it be in calmly quitting your job, when you could quit with style, and have an impressive story to tell your buddies later at the coffee shop?*

If Grandpa was looking for attention, he definitely had my attention as he was making quite the show of smashing through square bales and the swaths of straw laying across the field, waiting to be baled.

As Grandpa burst through the bales on that windy day, it looked like mini-bomb blasts going off, straight out of a movie. When the tractor hit the bales, it would blast them – sending them flying apart, flinging the straw everywhere and up into the air.

Grandpa, on his tractor, emerged from each cloud of straw like a victorious employee who was just set free from his mundane, dead-end job, and was sabotaging his boss's merchandise on his way out to greener pastures. But this is where things got confusing to me, Grandpa's work of sabotage was on his own work of freshly baled, square bales that had been baled only hours earlier, and they were now flying through the air in all directions.

When we finally met up with Grandpa, he stopped his tractor and jumped out. It was the fastest I had ever seen Grandpa move. We emerged from the car, which Mom had stopped just in front of Grandpa's tractor.

He yelled out, "The field's afire, down at that far-end! There's a wall of flames a-coming this-here way!"

Mom and I knew that word "fire" well. It was like a close kin. It was like a baby brother that would just show up, from time to time, in a basket on the front porch to give us some much-needed entertainment on a dull, boring day.

"Call that there fire department! Get as many people together quick as ya can, 'cause this fire's sure gonna be a beast with this high wind pickin' up. This fire's gonna erupt into sumthin' mighty nasty, if we don't move quick-like!" Grandpa shouted his instructions to Mom and me.

His words put cold chills down my spine and hot coals in the pit of my stomach, giving me a sick feeling inside.

Mom's voice weakly languished out, "OH, NO! Not another fire!"

"Yep! It's a fire, alright," Grandpa replied, as he began to climb back up into his tractor. "I ain't one to lie when there's a fire on the ground... maybe about your tea... but not 'bout a fire!"

He then went back in the direction that he had just come from, heading towards the fire that was just over the hill, which was currently obstructing our view of the blazing inferno.

Without a word more to say, Mom and I quickly jumped back into the car, and Mom raced out of the field, back to the farmyard to get the needed help.

Once in the car as we raced, bouncing over the uneven field, she then asked me, "What's wrong with my tea?"

I thought about it for a moment, then I

replied. "I think it's got to be too hot for his old gums 'cause he always blows on it first before he drinks it."

Back at the farmyard, Mom ran around the barnyard looking for her beloved husband, Elvis. After finding him in the barn, she informed Dad of the peril that was upon us.

Dad was not enthusiastic about this current fire; for he was not in any real mood for a fire fight, as his hands hadn't completely healed from earlier that summer when he had grasped the red-hot taps, which had been located on the burning fuel tanks, to turn them off.

I could hear Dad's voice sink to new depths of despair.

"Oh no! Ya've gotta be kidd'in me!" he groaned.

Fear and worry began to appear on his quivering lips, between his two thick, black, lamb-chop sideburns that had just barely grown completely back in, to their furry-thick glory after being singed clean-off while fighting the fire underneath the fuel tanks earlier that summer.

At a fast trot, Mom headed to the house to phone the fire department and the neighbours, for we would be needing their help once again.

As she opened the front door, she commanded. "Peter, you go round up your siblings and get ready to fight some fire. Find the shovels to stomp the fire with."

After I had rounded up my siblings, we kids raced to gather all the fire-fighting stuff.

Then Nedge, Calvin, and I, along with our older sisters, Zoey and Daisy, all piled into the pickup truck. Zoey, who was three years older than me and of driving age, drove us out to the field because she would not let me drive, even though I knew that I could drive into a field without running over anything or anybody.

By the time we got back out into the field, only fifteen minutes later - ready to begin the fire-fighting process - the field had turned into a raging fire. Fifty-mile-per-hour winds were violently whipping the back of the flames, much like a crazed carriage driver whipping the backs of his speeding, uncontrolled, galloping horses from the fiery abyss.

While Mom and I were gone, Grandpa had been blazing through the swaths, going back and forth in front of the raging inferno in an effort to slow down its pace. He was using the tractor and square baler like a plow to split the rows in half, the length of the field.

Catching up to us, Grandpa jumped out of the tractor and gave us kids some quick instructions before the bigger fire-fighting equipment would arrive.

"Now, listen up! I need ya kids to stay clear-away from the front of the wall of fire. Take them shovels and stomp out some of these smaller fires that are crawl'in along the back edges of the fire."

As Grandpa raced back to his tractor, we kids grabbed the shovels from the back of the pick-up truck. Then we headed over to where we could see some small fires still smoldering along the edge of the massive black patch in the field where the swathes of straw had been before the wind had sent the fire racing through them. We gave the small flames some good hard whacks with the back-side of the shovels. This method was effective in snuffing out the smoldering flames.

But our enthusiastic whacking soon petered out; and Daisy, Zoey, Nedge, Calvin, and myself ended up just standing around, yakking with each other. The fire wasn't really creeping along the ground all that fast in our minds. The small fires we were watching were creeping eastward, and the wind was blowing northward, so it was more of a slow-burning crawl. Every so often, this slow-moving fire would catch up to one of the un-burned square bales, laying in the field.

This created some excitement for a few minutes, as the bale would explode into a ball of flames on this hot and dry, windy day, causing us to add some, "Oooh's" and "Awww's" to the *poof* of a fiery bale.

Then our attention was drawn to where the real excitement was occurring farther up the field at the main fire. There, we could see quite a few of our neighbours, who were armed with shovels and pick axes beginning to congregate, as they tried to get in front of the flames to cut the head off the fiery beast.

And then we spotted a familiar vehicle that we kids knew all too well. We watched as the hog manure, vacuum truck pulled into the field, which turned out to be the saviour of the day. For that fresh, full load of liquid hog manure made the vacuum truck a real good, make-shift fire engine.

Once the truck driver started pumping out that manure, blasting the thick manure gravy onto the fire, it extinguished the fire with relative ease. The owner-operator of the manure spreader truck (who Dad hired from time to time to clean out our hog manure pits) had this timed nicely, as he laid a booby trap well in front of the flames. Once the fire got to that guck, it stopped dead in its tracks.

And any farmer or neighbour that was within a hundred yards of it just about fainted from the fumes. Clamping their hands over their noses and mouths, their eyes began watering from the stench of the manure gravy on that hot day. The sun's heat only magnified the potent aroma in the air.

These farmers and neighbours, though pleased that the dangers of the fire had been extinguished before it got into the standing barley crops just fifty feet away, didn't really have that look of overjoyed excitement on their faces that one would expect to see after watching the manure truck squash the neck of the raging inferno beast.

This fire-killing technique was so highly effective that I suggest they use this stuff in the fire trucks in the cities and at airports to stop a fire from eating up a building or a plane.

A tall neighbour choked out to the short neighbour, standing next to him, "Wow, that stuff really STINKS! LIKE... LIKE... WOW!"

The tall neighbour then fled in the opposite direction, trying to get away from the stench in front of him. He was holding a handkerchief over his nose, and was unaware that he was heading straight into another manure puddle, with his good town shoes on.

The manure truck driver, on the other hand, was wearing a grin that was as wide as the Saskatchewan River. He was the saviour of the day. He proudly stood there, holding the six-inch manure truck hose in his bare hands.

His immunity to the hog manure stench was not because of getting a booster shot at the doctor office, either. Nope. His immunity to the smell had been built up over time, with the odd mishap of the manure hose spraying over his body, speeding up his immunity process.

One example of when one of these little mishaps would sometimes occur, would be when he would have to blow the liquid hog manure back down into the manure pit in the barn. This was done to loosen up the harder manure that had settled down to the bottom of the pit once the liquid part of the manure had been pumped up into the truck. If the hard manure, which needed breaking up, was really hard, this process was like blasting water at a brick wall.

Like a tidal wave of liquid stench, the liquid manure would circle right back at the driver, who was holding onto the hose. The force of the pressure from the vacuum truck's pump was close to that of a jet's engine.

My dad had also experienced the true power of the vacuum truck's pump being used in reverse, and found it to be much like a high-powered fire engine with a six-inch hose nozzle.

My dad was a hog farmer; that was his trade. He made a living as most people do - one way or the other. Each job has it's benefits and drawbacks. The benefit of farming was that Dad could go hunting and fishing whenever he pleased. And one of the drawbacks was that the pigs created a lot of manure, which was collected into the large concrete pit beneath where the pigs stood in their holding pens. When the pit got full, Dad would give the vacuum truck driver a call, and get him to come and suck out all the manure with his vacuum truck.

The vacuum truck was a miraculous machine. It would very quickly suck up all the liquids that its hose's nozzle touched, but it had a limited ability in that it did not like to suck up large hard-packed solids. The hard-packed solids had to be blasted apart by the vacuum truck hose being used in reverse as a powerful blowing machine.

The first attempt, at cleaning out a manure pit for the first time with a vacuum truck, was the most interesting; for you would have to work out all of the kinks in your plan, which was made up on-the-fly, as you went along.

First, the vacuum truck driver puts the six-inch nozzle and hose down into a 45-degree, metal culvert that led from the outside of the barn into the pit that was underneath the hog pens that were inside the barn.

The second step was to suck out all of the liquid manure into the truck's large tank.

Step three: reverse the truck's vacuum from sucking in, to blowing out the liquids back down into the hole underneath the barn, and direct the liquids onto the encrusted solids, breaking them up into smaller chunks, which would then be sucked back up into the truck.

Step four: have the hog farmer double check, to make sure the hose is directed in the direction of the solids.

This is where Burt, who drove the big Mac truck, instructed my dad, "Okay, Elvis. I have it blowing back down into the hole at the hard-packed manure. You'd better double check and make sure the hose is pointed in the right direction."

Dad replied, "Al's-right, I'm a-goin'," as he

disappeared through the doorway into the barn.

Thirty seconds later, he reemerged from the barn, waving his arms and yelling at Burt. "Stop a-blowing! Stop a-blowing! Them liquids are's a-coming straight up out of the pit - like an uncontrolled geyser! It's a-tossing them pigs 'round in their pens! It's a-coming through the mesh floorin' underneath 'em! It's throwin' d'em through the air who are standin' on the mesh flooring. Whatta mess it's makin' in the barn! Whatta an ugly mess!"

After turning the blower off, Burt asked, "Well… then… what are we going to do?'

Contemplating the situation, Dad spoke, "Well… we've gotta go in there, get that hard stuff outta there." And then, after giving it another moment of thought, he said, "Okey-dokey, here's what we're gonna do. First, I'm gonna get that half-sheet of plywood from over there, and place it over the mesh floor. Then I'm gonna stand on that plywood. That way, them liquids will be redirected straight down onto that hard-packed manure. When I'm a-ready, I'll bang on the wall three times. That'll tell ya to starts a-blowing it back inside the barn. Then I'll give you another three raps if'en I needs ya to stop."

A couple minutes later, Dad had collected the half-sheet of plywood and disappeared back inside the barn with his plywood in hand. Soon we heard three distinctive bangs against the wall, coming from inside the barn.

At this point, Burt turned to me and said, "Perhaps you should go into the barn too, kid, just encase your dad needs your help."

"Okay," I said.

And as I made my way into the barn, I could hear my dad impatiently giving another three bangs to the wall.

Entering the barn, I could see that Dad was standing inside one of the pig pens, above the pit. He was standing on the square, 4-foot by 4-foot, half sheet of plywood that he had brought into the barn. He had placed the plywood down under his feet, on top of the mesh flooring. This plywood would stop the manure geyser from shooting upwards into the pen. My dad's weight would then securely hold the plywood down on the mesh flooring.

Then I heard the liquid blower on the vacuum truck start up. And with every action, there came an immediate reaction. The liquid manure that was inside the large septic tank on the back of the truck shot back down through the six-inch hose into the concrete pit. With a glorious force, the liquids blasted out the end of the hose nozzle. Slamming down against the bottom of the concrete pit, the manure gravy then quickly changed directions after hitting the bottom of the pit. Up the liquids came, shooting vertically straight upwards. They shot right through the mesh flooring, pounding the underside of the plywood that Dad was standing on. The powerful, pressurized liquids were making the plywood, underneath Dad's feet, lift and quiver.

The lifting increased in intensity, knocking Dad down onto his knees. As the blasting of the fluids grew by every second, Dad began clinging to one edge of the plywood with his finger tips, while gripping the other end of the plywood with the toes of his boots in an attempt to hold it down, at all cost. The plywood rose up a couple of inches off the mesh flooring, becoming a modern, magic crazy-carpet for farmers. Then the plywood started to spin, slowly at first. It turned around in circles like a top, with Dad still hanging on tightly - his finger tips and toes dug in deep, like a scared kitten stuck on a tree limb.

It was then that I heard the truck engine rev higher, as the driver pushed the throttle of the truck's blower up to maximum blowing power.

I knew this was not good, so I yelled out to Dad, "HANG ON, DAD, HANG ON!"

He looked up at me with a bewildered look on his face. He was like someone hearing a voice, but not hearing a word of English due to the noise of the geyser. Then the plywood with my dad on top of it, began to take flight from the force of the powerful geyser blast coming from underneath.

The power of this blast was obviously far more intense than Dad had anticipated. It lifted him six feet into the air, spinning him wildly - like the worst wild ride you've ever ridden on at the fairgrounds. This ride, that he was getting, was like the mechanical bull on steroids and set to level impossible. But what might seem to be impossible for normal individuals, was being conquered by my dad, Elvis.

Then he hollered out, "Stop the blower!" But Burt could not hear Dad's cries for help and kept on blowing the manure back down into the pit at full throttle.

I just stood there in stunned silence, watching. I was glued to the spot, scarcely believing what my eyes were beholding.

Dad then rode that sheet of plywood on the top of that geyser for a full-good ten to fifteen seconds before the instability of the flying plywood became too much for even the skillful talent level of my dad.

Then the sheet of plywood suddenly, without warning, flipped upside down, with Dad still clinging onto it. Looking like an opossum hanging from a branch, he clung to the underside of the plywood. Dad now took the full thrust of the geyser, as it pounded him squarely in his back. At this point, he gave up all hope of containing the flow of the dirty liquid. Releasing his grip on the plywood, the plywood sheet flew straight up through the air, hitting the ceiling of the barn, where it stay plastered by the geyser's flow monetarily.

Dad then rolled his way out of the powerful jet-stream flow that was mercilessly whipping him around from underneath. Just as he was about to reach safety, the plywood sheet slipped out of the geyser's flow. As gravity kicked back in, the plywood fell back down from the ceiling, landing on top of Dad. The plywood sheet flattened him to the floor of the barn, much like a flyswatter hitting the unsuspecting house fly.

As Dad then dragged himself out from under the plywood sheet, I heard him bellow out again, "S-stop the blower! Stop the blower!"

There was complete exhaustion in Dad's voice.

He crawled over to the barn wall and pounded on the wall three times, begging for Burt to stop the blower.

With that idea failing their expectations, Dad and Burt figured that the next time the pits needed cleaning out, they would come up with a better plan.

But as for now, with the pit cleaned out the best they could, Dad took a long soak in the bathtub to remove the strong unpleasant smell.

Back at the Field Fire

Some people have a built-up resistance to

the unpleasant smells of manure, much like how some mosquitoes seem to have a built-up resistance to mosquito dope. This liquid manure could easily be bottled and used as a spray to help others build up their immunity to the smell of hogs, and bring a smile back to their faces. It would be a slow process that would be worth it; but you may not be able to clean your shoes all that effectively or get a quick date for Saturday night.

After what felt like forever, perhaps two hours, Mom came out to see how we kids were doing; for she had been up at the other end of the field where the larger fire had been burning. As we watched her car approaching us, she seemed to be looking none too pleased at us. We could not understand her displeasure, for nobody was being burned up, and the pickup truck was still in one piece.

What could she possibly be upset about?

As she stopped the car and jumped out, she started running towards us, whipping square bales this way and that out of the way of the flames as two more bales burst into slow-moving flames. The bales were about ten feet apart in the rows, and were only about ten feet away from us.

Exasperated, Mom demanded, "Why are you kids not saving those square bales from burning up?!" as she whipped another bale out of the way.

It was at that moment, we kids looked at

each other and said, "Ohh, I get it! We need to save the bales also. We're here to save the square bales from the fire! Now, that makes sense! That sure would've saved us a lot of standing around, being bored."

Good thing she showed up to give us further instructions, I thought.

Nedge then ran over to one of the bales, which Mom had just tossed. And to make sure that it was at least five feet farther out of harm's way, he grabbed the bale by its strings and giving it a real mighty heave, he let it fly. The bale, taking flight, burst wide open into a cloud of straw.

Only a quiet, "Oops," escaped from Nedge's lips.

"Nedge, now just look at what you did! The bale's no good but for burnin' now," Mom said, with a groan.

Sheepishly, Nedge mumbled, "Sorry, Mom."

Mom then jumped back in the car, shaking her head as she raced back up the field to get the manure truck to come and finish the job.

We kids all then slowly turned around to stare at the field behind us. The field was littered with hundreds of blackened, smoking, burnt bales. Plumes of dark gray smoke rose out of each and every unsaved straw bale.

I then turned to my sister. "So, Zoey, how many of those bales do you suppose we could've saved?"

She responded, "Well... at least two in the

last thirty seconds, and probably lost over five hundred over the last two hours."

Chapter 3.

^

^ ^

Big Bucks
&
Jolly Scares

You will enjoy hearing about this event; some may even learn from this event – that scaring someone at the wrong moment can lead to calamity and unforeseen misfortune. Thankfully, this upcoming story did not cause my mom to outright drop dead from a heart attack. A little blunder in judgment like that would not have the great fun effect that a thrilling story should have. If it starts with fun; but ends in death, sadness, embarrassment, and a great deal of shame for an individual, it would then be never spoken of again.

Such was the case of the sad end of our Uncle Casper McVanBuck, who was at the ripe old age of a hundred-and-two. It was his heart that could not take one more pair of cold hands dashing out at him from the inside of his bedroom closet. The hands landed on his bare chest as he was getting ready for bed on Christmas Eve, as the villain bellowed out a loud booming, "GOT YA AGAIN, UNCLE CASPER! HA,HA,HA!" The icy-cold hands that had been previously cooled down in the snowbank outside of Uncle Casper's front door would normally strengthen the effect of the scare. In this case, it was a little too strong of an effect that was all done by the well-meaning hands of his loving McVanBuck kin.

Unfortunately, Uncle Casper didn't get to achieve one of his life-long dreams. As he stated on several occasions, "Now dying out in woods while being mauled to death by an enraged massive grizzly bear, with a hundred spectators watching me fight to my last breath at Yellow Stone National Park... this would be my claim to fame and glory."

Sometimes in life, we just don't get the glory we want.

Now, this coming, spectacular, unbelievable story and how it all transpired is secondhand information, for I was not present at the time of the event, due to me living out of province and having a young family of my own.

As for the parties in question here, to them the story that I wrote down is a completely different version. But I explained to them that the story is based on 100 percent of their truth and some of the secondhand McVanBuck information that I heard from Calvin, Nedge, and Mom.

A couple of years ago, it was the day before Thanksgiving. My brothers, who are avid hunters and outdoors men, were visiting at our parents' farmhouse. If you saw Calvin and Nedge, you would know them with the first glance. You'd see the whole nine yards: dressed in camouflage gear, old 4x4 pick-up trucks, and their gun cabinets jammed full with three-too-many guns than what the cabinet was designed to actually hold. Their wives nag them, all the time, to fix that problem by getting rid of some of their guns.

Now, personally, I don't have that problem myself anymore, after I bought a second gun cabinet, to hold my three-too-many guns.

Sitting around the kitchen table, my brothers were disputing who it was that had harvested the biggest whitetail-deer, antler rack during that fall's hunt. Nedge had brought his deer rack with him into the house, to show the rack off for all to see.

Calvin said, "My rack is a good half-inch taller than your rack. Sure...your rack is nice, but it's smaller. If you'd put your glasses on, you would see that clearly."

With shock in Nedge's voice, that Calvin would suggest that his rack was bigger, Nedge replied, "I agree that your rack might be a little, tiny bit taller; but my rack's a whole lot fatter, which makes it a whole lot bigger by far! ...Just look at the girth around the brow tines. I can't even get my hand around it."

Calvin then stood up quickly from the table. "I'll show you mine...they are right here in the basement!"

He then went downstairs to retrieve his trophy whitetail deer rack that may have even been harvested legally.

This way, Calvin and Nedge could simply get Dad to measure the racks out and score whose deer it was that was the bigger buck, without my brothers having to lock their racks together and fight to the death.

Moments earlier, Mom had also gone downstairs into the basement to retrieve a frozen turkey from the deep freezer.

Now, it was taking Calvin quite a long time to find his trophy buck deer antlers in the game room where he had temporarily stored them. Mom, seeing the antlers a few minutes earlier, had figured them to be just one of Dad's deer racks, and she had put Calvin's rack in the storage room in the basement

that contained the large mound of other deer antlers and moose racks, which Dad had accumulated over the past fifty years of hunting big game animals.

While Calvin looked for his missing rack, Mom had gotten her turkey out of the freezer and began to carry it up the stairs.

This turkey was one of the largest frozen turkeys known to mankind. It was the King Kong of all frozen turkeys. Since my parents raise their own turkeys, it was not out of the realm of possibilities to get a 50-pound bird; for nobody was going to go hungry in my mother's house at Thanksgiving time. Then we would all get to stuff down the mountain of Thanksgiving turkey, until the next giant turkey was crammed into the oven, two months later at Christmas.

Nedge, growing impatient while he waited for Calvin to come back up from the basement, thought that he would see what was taking him so long. But before Nedge could take a look down the stairway, for the stairs were behind a wall, he could hear footsteps coming up the stairs.

Believing the footsteps to be Calvin coming up from the basement, Nedge thought it would be a good time to give Calvin a friendly little scare at the top of the steps. So he quickly hid behind the stairway wall.

You could give somebody quite a good scare in this particular location. When we were kids, we had spooked each other quite effectively in this key location, many times.

Nedge felt the urge of a good old-times' memory flooding back to him, like a long-lost puppy happily coming home after a long time away from his master. Nedge felt it would be a good time to brush up on the old scare trick at the top of the stairs for old times' sake, and set alight some good memories, once again.

Nedge quietly crouched down behind the wall that paralleled the stairway. This blocked his view of the person coming up the stairs, whom he suspected was Calvin. And at the right moment, when he heard that the footsteps were almost at the top of the stairs, he leaped up from his crouched position - jumping out from behind the stairway wall, like a wild leopard hiding behind some bushes in the wilds of Africa, then leaping out in front of the unsuspecting water buffalo.

Nedge roared, *"Rowwererrr!"* loudly as he extended his hands up above his head, looking like orangutan casting his frightening dance upon his surprised, unprepared victim.

Mom had been slowly making her way up the stairs, groaning out a few soft *rrrs* and grunts and sweating as she cradled the heavy mammoth-sized frozen turkey, like a giant frozen bolder, in her arms.

On the second-to-the-last top step, she saw a wild man flash out from behind the wall. This terrifying wild man was producing a

loud *Rowwerr-ha-ha-ha* sound.

Nedge danced and bellowed, dangling his fingers and hands above his head like a dancing, stringed, wooden puppet at the top of the stairway. Nedge was flapping his tongue out of his mouth, wagging it from side to side, all the while shaking his head. He rolled his eyes around in his head, to make the whole scene have the maximum effect possible on Calvin.

With a fearful howl, Mom screamed, "BLAAAAAGGGGAAA!" as she broke into a fox-trot right there on the step, like a heavy big horned sheep gracefully dancing on a narrow mountain ledge. She then launched the 50-pound turkey straight up into the air with ease, even with most of her strength sucked out of her.

Like a cannonball let loose from the basket of a medieval catapult, the frozen turkey flew way up into the air, above Nedge's head.

This caught Nedge quite by surprise as he was expecting to see Calvin with the deer antlers, and not our aging Mom at the top of the stairs!

The turkey came down onto Nedge, as he did not react soon enough to catch the beast with his arms and hands, even though they were above his head. The turkey slipped right through his arms, and came straight down onto the top of his head. Nedge's neck sank down like a shrinking spring, and his legs buckled out like a first-time skater hitting the ice.

Nedge had two things going in his favor that spared his life: one was that he had a head that was as solid as a millstone in strength and physics; the second was that as the turkey pushed down on Nedge's head, it also pushed him away from the stairs, preventing him from falling down the stairs with the bird.

As Nedge's knees buckled, they built up energy like that of a tightly-coiled spring underneath his body. When his knees released themselves, he shot the bird off his head downwards, straight back at Mom!

Sure, the bird gave Nedge a good-sized bump on the top of his head, but nothing he couldn't shake off in six to eight months of severe migraine headaches. Unfortunately for Mom, Nedge did not catch the flying turkey in his arms, as his outstretched arms had first implied.

The turkey, in turn, went straight back towards Mom by way of Nedge's wicked headbutt, like you would see a soccer star hammering a soccer ball towards a goalkeeper in a net. But this was not a soft soccer ball, this was a heavy block of ice and frozen flesh coming at full speed towards Mom.

Now, Mom did not have as quick of reflexes at the age of sixty as she once had, but she did make an attempt to catch the flying bird in her arms to save the turkey from falling back down the stairs. But it was not like catching a loose, flying, pet parrot in her arms.

She blurted out, "Oh no! My turkey!" as the bulk of frozen bird slammed hard into her stomach as if it was trying to go through her like a charging bull.

"*OOF!*" she sputtered out, with a forced plume of air.

As the frozen cannonball plowed into her, she tumbled backwards all the way back down the stairs with the frozen turkey bouncing off of her multiple times.

Before she hit the bottom of the steps, the turkey stomped onto her chest and then bounced off of her buttocks, before leaping over her cartwheel-spinning body. It then raced ahead of her to the finish line at the bottom of the steps, just in time to ricochet off of the back wall. The turkey then spun back like a frozen curling stone to catch Mom at the bottom of the stairs, in its frozen wings - to lovingly help soften her final landing. She landed squarely on her back on top of the round, spinning bird, her back making a loud frightening *crack* sound.

The spinning bird, that was going a hundred miles per hour after accumulating this vast amount of speed as it tumbled down the stairs through gravity, whirled Mom off as quickly as she had arrived.

Mom cried out, "Whaaaag!"
As she flew off the top of the spinning frozen

carcass, like a kid being tossed from the merry-go-round at the schoolyard, she was slammed up against the back wall at the bottom of the stairway, leaving her in a bruised and broken heap.

There was silence for a few breathless moments, except for the spinning whirl of the turkey that was still winding itself out of its high-speed spin, as Calvin and Nedge raced to Mom's aid.

Kneeling down beside her, Nedge worriedly cried out, "Mom, speak to me... Mom, speak to me. Is anything broken!?!" as he gently slapped her cheeks to get her to come back to earth and step away from the light at the end of the tunnel.

She then groaned out as she came to, "Maybe... ohh... but... is the turkey alright?"

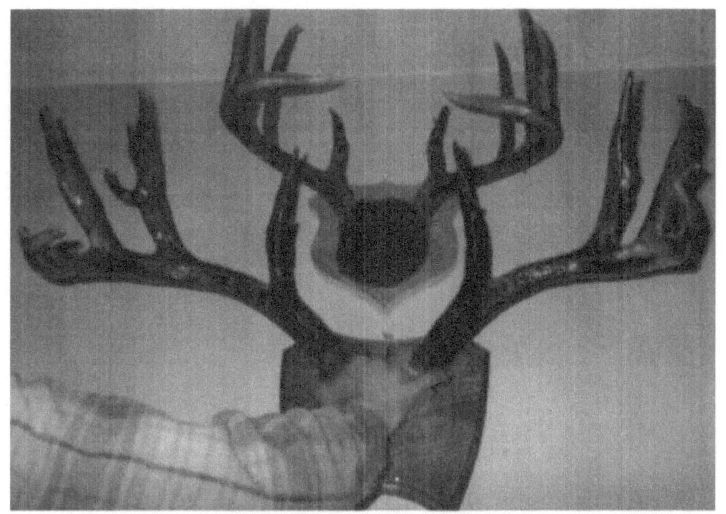

Chapter 4.

^ ^

^ ^

Otis & the Bees

...& a Wanna-be 3-Star General

Buzz, buzz went the hornet in my ears as it flew around my head, before I felt its unpleasant stings.

"Ouch! That hurts a lot more than I remember," I said to Joy, my wife, as we worked in our garden and a large hornet stung me without warning. "That really smarts!"

"Did something get you?" Joy inquired, looking up from the weeds she was pulling, to see me rubbing the back of my neck.

"Ya, a massive black-and-white hornet just nailed me three times, like a jackhammer!"

"Oh no, please just keep it away from me," she requested, as her eyes darted about, looking in the air for any potential, future assaults that might be directed towards her.

Then looking about the garden for my children to warn them to watch out for the incoming attacker, I noticed that our children were no longer weeding in the garden, but were now in the barnyard throwing a flurry of stones at a paper hornet hive that was situated in the rafters of the cow shed.

"Well, that explains where the bees are coming from, Joy," I said.

As I rubbed the back of my neck and watched as my children abruptly fled away from the now-enraged hornets, memories flooded my mind. I was about ten years old again, and that summer was an extremely hot and dry one at the McVanbuck farm.

With the hot and dry weather, it provided the perfect conditions for the dreaded black-and-white hornets and the black-and-yellow paper wasps to flourish. There were paper hornet nests everywhere. Big ones, small ones – in trees, in the ground, and a nest was even found in one of our toy sandbox trucks. The hornets would just fly in and out the truck's windows... they would chase me even when I wasn't trying to play with it.

Another hornet hive that we boys found, was literally in the cavity of a dead chicken carcass. This hen had mysteriously died – perhaps from old age or perhaps from the fright of being chased by our city cousins.

Some of our city cousins, like Eugene, were odd creatures, for they would chase our chickens with a great deal of excitement and pleasure, as if they had never seen a chicken before.

This chicken carcass, with the hornet hive in it, had fully perished, withered, and dried to a crisp in the hot sun. The excessive dryness had turned the carcass into a chicken mummy, without it even decomposing. The hornets flew in and out of their paper hive's front door, right where the chicken's kazoo would have been. They had brilliantly renovated the carcass, and converted it into their five-star, luxury condo. At least, the mummified carcass hadn't completely gone to waste.

Now, not far from my parent's house, there were also two very large paper hives built into the walls of an old wooden granary, which was no longer in use. The paper hives extended to the outside of the granary wall through two finger-sized knotholes. The black-and-yellow wasps used one knothole as their front door.

And about eight feet away from the wasps' knothole to the west, was the hornet family's

front porch. These relatives of the wasps were the much larger, black-and-white-striped hornets. Both hive entrances were approximately three feet off the ground and were on the same south-facing wall of this granary.

Nedge, Calvin, and I were now off from school and into our much-needed summer holidays, but we were in need of some entertainment to keep our morale up, as we baked in the hot sun. We were really hankering for something with a bit more thrill to it; something with a bit of a sting to it – to test our courage, wits, strength, and our blind stupidity.

Then Nedge suggested, "Hey, come to think of it, why don't we mess with those bees in that granary? Maybe we can throw some gravel at them!"

I enthusiastically responded, "Yeah! Good idea, Nedge. And I'll be the ruling 3-Star General!"

"What about some sticks?" Calvin chimed in, "Maybe we can bat some rocks at the bees?"

"Or just bat the bees with the sticks!" said Nedge.

We three boys approached this irresistible itch for the up-coming action in a military manner. I would be their 3-Star General, due to me being the oldest, and my duty was to implement a self-imposed, higher rank. The enemy would be the far-too-jolly bunch of bees on this hot day.

The first task was to find some sticks in the nearby woods – some good clubbing-sized sticks, roughly an inch in diameter and about two to three feet long. These sticks would serve as the weapons of choice to give these bees the beat-down we felt that they deserved, while at the same time, give them a fighting chance to dodge our swinging sticks.

Once back at the granary with our chosen sticks in hand, we quickly decided that we would start at the front door of the black-and-white hornets. It only took a couple of taps to the wall with our bee sticks to get a few hornets stirred up. Like super-fighter jets taking to the air from the deck of an aircraft carrier, the hornets came zooming out from the knothole in the wall, one at a time. To see the hornets, charging out of their nest with a significant amount of anger, was a real delight to us; they would, indeed, be the real contender that we were looking for.

Nedge proclaimed, "If it's a fight they want, then a fightin' is what we're gonna give them!"

When the first wave of angry hornets zoomed out, well-armed with their long stingers, we thought these to be the front-line, guarder hornets. They were much larger and slower than their paper-wasp cousins, so with some batting skills of a major leaguer baseball star, we would club them out of the air to the ground.

This was quite an exhilarating thrill, as it would send adrenaline shooting into our veins like a super serum.

If our swing missed, we would often get a bonus dose of hornet venom flowing into our veins, which would be followed by us yelling, "Ouch! That stings! How dare you sting me!? Take that..." *thwack* "and that..." *thwack*.

With a fast swing and a good eye, one could connect that stick with the hornets like a ball to a bat; then you would hear a little *pop* noise, which would create some "oohs" and "awwwes" from the cheering crowd.

But if we missed the zooming hornet, which was more times than not, they would do quite the number on us. And instead of hearing "Oohs!" and "Awwwes," you would hear, "Y-a-ouch! That burns!"

And sometimes you would hear a heavy *clunk,* closely followed by Nedge saying, "Ouch! Hey, guys! Watch where you're swingin' your bee-sticks!" while Nedge would rub the growing goose egg on the top of his head from a miss-guided stick.

Then Calvin or I would have to say, "Sorry, Nedge... your head was in the way of a great big hornet that was about to land on you... but good news, we killed it!"

When a hornet did get us, it was more of a flailing of the hands, while at the same time, being on the run away from the granary.

This type of black-and-white hornet could

sting with a real punch and with the rapid-fire of multiple stings. Getting stung was like a runaway sewing machine punching into our skin. This intensity was mainly due to the fact that the hornet did not have his butt fall out from his backside after the first sting, as honeybees do.

The thrills of this entertainment were most exciting to us boys, and it had our adrenaline running at full capacity.

We would be frantically swinging our bee sticks in no set, technical direction, at this point. With our heads darting in all directions, our legs would be shifting gears into a full-out run.

If the hornets began to get the upper-hand on us and started to lay a beat-down on us in packs of twenty or thirty with their fearsome stingers, then we would have to leg-it out of there fast.

It was up to me, being the 3-Star General, to halt the retreat.

I would yell out, "No risk, no reward men! Now, into battle, men! CHARGE!"

You could not have seen happier smiles on our faces. There were grins upon our faces from ear to ear; and welts upon our heads - here and there. We would tap the wall and lay a few hornets to death with our makeshift bats, until the stings of the day were too much to bear. The next day, we would be back again, swinging at the wasps with our bee sticks. This carried on for several days.

After the first few raids, I had realized that it would be to my advantage to command my troops from a distance rather than heading into battle with them.

Now, the eradication process of Calvin and Nedge swatting the hornets from the air, had became relatively effective, with me commanding the troops. After a couple of days had passed with us carrying out our daily raids, it came to the point where we could see a significant difference in how many hornets came out of the wall when Calvin or Nedge tapped on it. We were winning the war with my excellent military mind, but this method had its military drawbacks – particularly on heavy sting days.

My feeble troops, Nedge and Calvin, complained, "We can't take any more stings!"

They wanted to completely retire for the day with the sun still high in the sky – after only enduring seven or eight bee stings each. My troops felt that their treatment by their drill sergeant was somehow unjust, or something like that. They had a great deal of anger in their voices as they would be scratching at their latest stings, either on their throats, ears, swollen eyelids, or wherever the red welt would be currently growing.

It was most unfortunate if the hornets got both eyes, for that would set the war back for at least a day. It would be, at this point, that I would have to remind the troops to just keep their anger focused on the true enemy – the hornets – even if they could not see the hornets anymore. Once both eyelids were stung, and temporary blindness was starting to settle in, there was little point in telling them where to direct their anger, it was better to just give them a direct order.

"Calvin, just attack in the direction where the loudest buzzing sounds are coming from!" I commanded.

This is where things could get dangerous for my own self, even if my men's eyes were only red swollen slits.

I did my best to bring understanding and wisdom to my troops with the fact that it was not my fault that I had only two or three stings. I tried reasoning with them that it was a well-established military strategy that if there were no soldiers for me to command – from a distance into battle – then I would not have a job as a general and a military pension... which they had no idea what a pension was, and neither did I, but it is to the advantage of being a superior military mind to not know what you are talking about.

If I could not reason with my troops to stick with the war for that day, even when I suggested that perhaps they needed me to give them a whack with my bee stick on their backsides for some needed incentive... and when it looked like the two of them, united with mutiny on their minds, would be soon giving me a beat-down with their bee sticks, I quickly decided to give the troops a much-needed military day pass.

It was about the second week into our military campaign, that our cousin Otis came over to our house for a visit. After showing Otis all of our recent exploits around the farm that we had been up to that summer, we then gravitated towards the most exciting entertainment of the summer – the hornets that were coming out of those knotholes in the grain bin.

Nedge, Calvin, and myself, grabbing up our sticks that we had been using for the hornets' daily beat-down, went looking for a stick for Otis to use. It's one of those odd things in life, that when you need that extra stick, it's just nowhere to be found, especially on short notice. We, however, were able to find a two-by-four board that was about three feet long that was holding the door closed to Dad's granary, which was full of barley.

Otis asked, "But... but, won't your dad get angry with all his grain pouring out onto the ground?"

"Nah," Calvin replied. "Those few handfuls can feed a few deer. Our dad loves the deer."

And we walked away from the now-growing pile of barley pouring out of the granary's doorway.

As Nedge handed the two-by-four to Otis, he explained, "The two-by-four is a bit bigger, but it'll definitely get more wasps per swing than our skinny sticks."

Otis replied with a frown, "This board's a piece of junk!"

We were now all well-armed, like four thugs. We set our plan into action by tapping on the wall of the black-and-white hornets as usual. To our disappointment, nobody came out... not one single hornet.

Perhaps the whole hornet family had been eradicated, or maybe they had simply abandoned their home and the hornets had gone somewhere else.

With confusion, Calvin then put his eye right up to the knothole to look into the darkness to make certain that no one was home and announced, "Nope, I can't see any hornets in there... it's black in there... wait! I see something..."

Then came that surprising, "YE-OUCH! He got me!" as a lone hornet had found an easy target staring right through his front door at him.

This lone hornet must have overslept when his family packed their luggage and left to find a safer location to live.

As Calvin tried to stretch open his eyelid that was slowly clamping his eye shut, a few uncontrolled tears trickled down his face... these were not crying tears though, but were army, tough guy, hornet-sting type of tears.

I suggested that he should have put his finger into the hole first and then wiggled it around a little bit, before looking inside to see if it was clear of hornets.

At first, this hornet made us all leap into full ready-to-swing mode; but it was only false hope, for that lone stray hornet was the last to come out of the knothole.

Even though we were disappointed that no one was home, we were not in despair as our attention was drawn to the feared, black-and-yellow wasps who lived next door, eight feet away. This was a new challenge, that when tangled with, would not disappoint; for this hive in the wall had been thriving and growing in numbers for weeks.

With sinister grins on our faces, we approached the wasp hive with our clubs in our hands. We were ready to go toe-to-toe with the formidable foe.

Suddenly, I yelped out in pain, "Oucheeee!" as a welt began growing on my nose. One of the wasp's scouting parties had spotted us earlier than expected and had nailed me before fleeing back into his hive like a coward to warn the others.

The wasp named Jack would've yelled out to his ten thousand brothers and sisters, "Mayday! Mayday! Humans are on the war path and are closing-in fast upon us!"

Then Sue, one of his sisters, replied in disbelief, "No way! Are they the two fool jackals from earlier this summer?"

Jack answered, "No, and their army has doubled in size! Now, there's four of them, and they're coming well-armed, with sticks. And they have a half-wit, 3-star General in charge."

Then Sue questioned, "Do those fools know who they are dealing with?"

Jack responded, "Yes, but I think that they've been out in the hot sun too long."

Then the hive exploded with rage as the gossip mill roared at full speed through the hive in seconds.

The truth was that we had been keen to avoid this nasty hive of wasps. This was because prior to this engagement, earlier that summer, our other cousin Eugene and I had thrown several gallons of used tractor oil on the wasps' hive door. This attempted assault did not cut down on their massive numbers as we had hoped, but it did seem to enrage them significantly; which had sent us fleeing for our lives, as we tried our best to avoid the rapid, machine-gun fire pounding down on us.

Another reason for us not being particularly fond of the wasps was that these warrior bees had a real tenacity about them. They had twice the speed of the slower, bigger black-and-white hornets, and they had at least five times the agility-rate in being able to change directions at full speed. These bees had some serious anger issues also, which Eugene and I had experienced firsthand.

We could see the remaining evidence of the first attack by the empty oil can that still rested right where we'd dropped it in our haste, a mere foot from the wasps' front gate of their fortress.

Neither of us had been willing to retrieve the oil container because – it was not my job as a 3-Star General, and Eugene was a yellow-bellied, cowardly private. Perhaps it was the measure of defeat these bees had instilled in us that had made Eugene and me go for an easier target... the lame hen turkey and the other two speedy, zigzagging turkeys.

So now, as Otis, Nedge, Calvin, and myself set out our plan of attack, there were some noticeable differences other than the bees' upgrades in speed, agility, and intelligence. One was the wasps' sheer massive volume of numbers, for they were zooming in and out of the wall at a pretty feverish pace, and that was even without giving a few taps to the wall. What made these guys also a bit different, was that they would go after you – even without being provoked and antagonized.

After giving the wall its initial couple of taps, there was no need for the third tap. The volume of buzzing coming from inside of the wall tripled in strength, as the humming of the swarm grew into a roar. Then the wasps came pouring out of the wall, like a stream of milk out of a milk-jug – but one that defied the laws of gravity, as they turned into quite the black cloud above our heads.

This made us all retreat to a safer distance

of about thirty yards away to regain our wits, get our focus, and come up with a simple plan. We rubbed at the new stings that we had just received.

"Okay, boys, we've got a new plan," I announced as I squatted down and drew the shape of a granary in the gravel with my stick. "This is gonna get a little hairy. We had best attack these bees one person at a time. That way, when one guy goes in swinging and has to run for his life, the other three guys can pat and swat away the layer of bees off of the retreating, brave, bloodthirsty warrior... if need be."

Nedge piped up, "How about the 'Stop, Drop, and Roll' method?"

This was what he had learned in school when extinguishing a fire that is on a person.

In one accord, we quickly agreed, "Yah! Right on, Nedge, that's the way! It's a good idea."

So with that, I instructed, "Okay, Calvin, you're up first. You're the youngest, and we think you might even be the quickest. Now, if things get too intense in there, you just leg-it out of there quick. I figure that we could see some top-flight, running speeds today... if all goes well."

And with that, Calvin shook his head from side to side, then sprang into action and started in. He began swinging his bee stick some ten feet before he reached the menacing cloud of wasps, which were flying around in a highly-agitated, aggressive manner.

As he ran forward, he yelled out, "DIE, EVIL B-E-E-E-E-S!"

Then, within a flash, Calvin was suddenly on the retreat, and he was now yelling out, "A-A-A-A-H!"

He was at a full run, legging-it out of there with a towering, black cloud of bees chasing after him. The towering black cloud was much bigger than first anticipated. Calvin was running straight towards us with what looked like maybe fear or excitement on his face, but it was so hard to see clearly with so many bees in the way.

Seeing Calvin fleeing in our direction, I quickly decided that I needed to make a military adjustment. I could no longer help in swatting the bees off of Calvin, but instead, I needed to lead the troops in a 200-yard run away from Calvin and his new-found pack of friends that were savagely clinging to his back and head.

Once we all had pretty much cleared the cloud of aggression that had been chasing Calvin, who somehow had managed to out race us, we regrouped after being scattered about in all directions. And as a great army general in the military strategy of "divide-and-conquer," I sent in the next volunteer private.

It was Nedge's turn. Now, Nedge wasn't as fast as Calvin, but he had more back muscle;

so I figured that he would be able to carry the pack of wasps more easily.

Without asking a single question, Nedge raced into battle, hollering something that sounded like, "Arrm-a-ar-har! How dare you attack my brother, you heartless kamikazes!"

His method of swinging was a bit unorthodox, for he was swinging his bee stick over his head, like it was a helicopter blade. Perhaps he felt that since most of the wasps were dive-bombing him from above, these bees would get messed up in his helicopter's propeller.

This might have even worked, had there only been a single army attacking from above. But it was the bees that were coming in from the four other directions which brought in an extra twenty-million bees, in this single military attack on Nedge. They were laying a heavy sting-count upon his body, but with Nedge's sharp mind, he executed his plan. He stopped... dropped... and rolled.

It would have been a bit wiser, I might add, if Nedge had done the dropping and rolling part a little farther away from the hive than a mere two feet. His rolling, break-dancing moves didn't last long though, as he spun wildly on the ground – looking like a fly spinning his last after being sprayed by a can of Raid.

At this moment, Nedge also made some military adjustments to his plan; for we were, at that moment, yelling at him that it was now time to leg-it. And with that, he leapt off the ground and legged-it.

We all watched, transfixed for a moment, for being the big boy that Nedge was, he was really movin' it, as the cloud of bees behind him appeared to be growing in strength. It became a violent tornado of bees with a deafening hum. And with that, we all turned and ran some 300 yards away.

The only real disappointment I had, as Nedge made his hasty retreat, was that he did not think to pick up Eugene's and my empty oil container while he was so close to the hive. This lack of forward thinking was regrettable and would need swift military discipline with my bee stick to Nedge's backside. But upon closer observation, I realized that showing military discipline at a time of dropping military morale wouldn't be advisable. I would have to show self-restraint and spare him the rod... just this once.

It was then that Otis spoke up with his helpful suggestion, "Nedge, maybe you should've had long pants on, instead of your shorts."

We stared down at Nedge's legs that were covered in red welts. They looked much like a teenager who's been hit real hard with puberty and has a healthy crop of pimples all over their legs, though I would think Nedge would have welcomed the crop of pimples, at this point, compared to the number of stings inflicted upon him.

Nedge, now defeated, muttered aloud, "Them teachers can't be trusted for nothing... the 'Stop, Drop, and Roll' doesn't put out the burning flames of the wasp stings!" as he rubbed his legs with his hands.

Attempting to encourage Nedge, Calvin spoke up, "At least your 'Stop, Drop, and Roll' showed us some pretty good-looking, break-dancing moves."

After taking a few minutes to regain our fearless focus, we noticed that the massive black swarm lording over us seemed to be making their last defensive stand in front of the granary. They appeared to be taunting us and even daring us to give them yet another "go" at their well-armed defensive position. We were suffering some painful set-backs in our eradication attempts at this point, but we weren't without military personnel waiting to be pushed into the war, for we still had a chance to win against the odds.

Calvin, looking like he'd stepped into the boxing ring with a pro-boxer for a spell with his eye now swollen completely shut, reminded us, "Hey, guys, remember the story of the Yankees at the Alamo... two Canadians fought them off and won against fifty thousand Americans... we can win too!"

I was going to correct his history errors, but then thought to myself, while an eerie silence hung in the air – for even the wasps seemed to freeze in mid-flight for a moment while they took a few history notes - but there was no point bringing down the military morale any farther.

Instead, I cried out, "Y-A-A-AH, Calvin! Onward, Canadians... fight the Alamo to the last wasp!"

There were still two guys to have a "go" – myself and Otis. Otis had the nicer, bigger stick...and logic told me that a bigger stick was better at killing large packs of wasps per swing... if all went favorably for Otis.

In reality, things looked bleak, unless a crop-duster arrived soon, filled full with a pesticide and sprayed the swarm from above. With not a plane in the sky coming to our rescue anytime soon, we all focused on Otis. His lips started to quiver, as he looked at Nedge and Calvin, with their badly stung up faces. They were staring back at him.

Now, Otis really didn't want to have a "go". In fact, he had a lot of fear in his eyes. He would need some military motivation to bring down the Alamo.

So Calvin, Nedge, and I started to encourage him by saying, "Come on, Otis! Go for it. You're a real tough fighter. You can do this!" and "Don't be ridiculous, they're not going to bite you... they're only going to sting you... besides, their stingers don't stay in you like the honey bee stingers do. You can hardly feel the stings... if the stings are piled up on top of each other."

Eventually, we just started chanting,

"Get'em, Otis. Get'em, Otis. Get'em, Otis."

We weren't much in the way of being singers, but it was a catchy tune and we put our whole hearts into our new military chant.

After some five minutes of prodding and goading, Otis overcame his fears of the wasps; and to our great delight, he charged into action.

Now, it appeared to us that Otis had no real plan at all... probably due to the paralyzing juice of fear that he was drinking on. He tightly grabbed his two-by-four board, placing one sweaty hand on each end of the three-foot long plank. Then he set his forehead in the middle of the board, while keeping one hand at each end of the plank. Then he just started running straight towards the swarm on the granary wall. The board on Otis' forehead looked like the horns on the head of a raging bull on a full-out charge. There wasn't any real batting action; Otis was just running straight towards the hive, as we stood watching from a safe distance.

A thick layer of wasps had accumulated around the hive's hole in the wall. They were maybe three or four wasps thick in this location, clinging to the wall like the last resistance band of patriots that had yet to become airborne. It was quite the sight to see, as we saluted Otis to most certain peril and a massacre.

So, at a full-out run, Otis crashed into the granary wall, head first, with that two-by-four board landing square in the middle of the thickest layers of wasps. Otis, without a doubt, killed at least a hundred – maybe even two hundred of the wasps – with this single head-on assault.

This swarm, crawling out of the hive, was unbelievably large. The swarm in the air was growing to a massive scale, and the whole yard was now filled with a humming roar. There were angry bees in all directions. They were like snipers, sitting on every tree leaf. And they speckled the air like a hurricane full of tiny pebbles... pebbles with angry brains and large stingers.

I reckoned, at this point, that this once-confined military assault had aroused every bee in every one of those smaller hives scattered around the yard, and had enlisted them to join in on the fight against us humans. There were so many wasps, hornets, and bees... they were getting stuck in my hair and ears. I even had to spit a few out of my mouth.

Otis was still smashing violently against the wall, when his pants dropped down to his knees. Using only one hand, now, to hold onto his two-by-four board that was covered black by the wasps, this brave soldier was trying to crush the wasps to death by pinning them underneath the board, against the wall. His other hand was flailing around in the air, trying to remove the now-exceedingly aggressive, angry swarm that was stinging him everywhere. At the same time, he was trying to pull up his pants that had worked their way down. Otis was a fighter and was undaunted by the great deal of stings... or maybe, it was that he was just having a hard time getting his pants back up with one hand.

He was not making a normal retreat or dropping his two-by-four board, either, to get his pants up. Even his uncontrolled yelling was off tune, like he was in some form of delusional shock. His once happy fun, that he had been having with us, was now turning into madness!

Now, as Otis was flailing away at the wasps, the house door opened and his dad, Uncle Jake, emerged from the house along with my parents.

They stood on the porch, in stunned silence for a moment, before Uncle Jake demanded, "What the-e-e.... heck are you boys doing...?!? Those bees are WASPS! Otis, get away from them!... wasps don't give you honey. Get away from them, this is a bad thing!"

My Uncle Jake was a smart man. His mind would be thinking that there must be a good, l-o-g-i-c-a-l explanation for his son to be covered in a thick layer of wasps and yelling, with his pants down around his knees. His boy – his first-born son – was reenacting a child's cartoon.

The three adults kept yelling, "Run! Get out of there, Otis! Just run away!" as they stared in amazement and bewilderment, as to why we were trying to collect honey from a wasp hive, for there was no apparent reasoning for this madness in their eyes. The wasps then began stinging Uncle Jake and my parents.

One would have figured with all the flailing, kicking, and yelling that Otis was doing, that the wasps would have gotten scared and left him alone sooner or later, but they were stubborn. One would have thought that they weren't just stinging him, but maybe they really were also biting wasps... boy, did he ever know it.

Then my uncle's voice cracked in the air like a whip. It sent chills up and down our spines. His voice thundered out of his mouth with a shriek that killed several thousand wasps right in front of his face, just by the pounding shock-wave of dread to their untrained ears.

He bellowed, "OTIS!... GET IN THE TRUCK, BOY! NOW!"

With that, Otis' mind snapped out of its haze, as a new layer of fear and bravery came upon his face when he heard his dad's voice. He dropped the two-by-four board, pulled up his pants, and then bolted for their pickup truck.

It was like the shock-wave of his dad's voice had broken off the stunned madness. It was a much-needed jolt, for Otis seemed to leave ninety percent of the wasps behind, as he now raced towards his dad's pickup truck.

Uncle Jake did not stand there on the porch for long, to swat at the multiple stings being inflicted upon his back, head, legs, and everywhere else skin grew on his large frame. He had been abandoned by my parents, who had retreated into the safety of their house. Uncle Jake fled for the safety of his truck to escape the evil swarm of dive-bombers from the air. My normally fearless uncle, who was a tall man at six-foot-five, had a great deal of what appeared to be fear growing on his face as he kept swatting at the bees, this way and that, as he made his way to his truck.

As Otis climbed into the truck with him, he could be heard protesting, "But, Pops! I was having such good fun! Why do we have to go home now?... things were just getting good!"

And he began rubbing at the great many welts covering his body.

Otis was layered thick with a great number of military badges for honour and bravery. These red swelling badges of honour that littered his entire body were on display, for all to gaze upon with "ow's" and "oh's" for days after.

Following that memorable day, for some strange reason, we did not see Otis again for the rest of that summer. He must have gotten real busy reading or something... but at least, he had left happy that day, with a great military feat attempted.

Chapter 5.

^ ^

^ ^ ^

Wing a Zinger

Today, there is only a single large farmer where there once was a great army of small farmers, who farmed the flat prairie lands of Canada. In the past, these small farms were tended by tough, mean farmers who were really strong, stout, and solid, like round steel grain bins. Their husbands were pretty tough as well.

The farmers of yesterday were really tough, and I am not talking about the ability to sit on a solidly frozen, wooden outhouse seat with bare buttocks at minus 40-degrees Celsius and not even wince. I mean tough, as in being tough enough to avoid bankruptcy, year after year, for some 40-plus years.

To a good many farmers, the word "bankruptcy" is to be avoided, just like the words "Death," "The Grave," and "Bankers" are to be avoided. To the farmer then, bankruptcy should be avoided for as long as one can possibly bear... or at least until spring when the next farm relief kicks in again with the yearly crop insurance.

Farm bankruptcy can also be avoided if you have a kid playing pro hockey in the NHL. The hockey kid, making the big bucks, can then lend you a couple million, so you can make it through one more winter. And just maybe, there would be enough money leftover, after paying the bank back, to put in one of those indoor flushing toilets, at least that is according to my neighbour, Mr. Brown.

Grandpa McVanBuck used to say to my dad, "Elvis, ya want to own your very own farm someday, just like your old man?... then skate ten more of them laps 'round that rink. What'd ya say, kid?... your feet are cold, and you can't feel your hands anymore?

"What's wrong with you?... it's only minus 36-degrees Celsius out here at the pond... we're not even in the wind. Pro-hockey scouts are lookin' for farm kids that are

tough.

"Now get going, ten more laps... then practice shootin' a hundred more hockey pucks.

"What do you mean cold? Quit crying... let me see... yep, white fingers are a bad sign of frostbite. Okay, okay... you only need to do two more laps and skip the puck shootin' until tomorrow, when the weather warms up to minus 30-degrees Celsius... Cripes, a heat wave's a-comin' in... just think of how many laps you can do then!"

If a farm kid did not make it to the NHL, due to all of his fingers freezing off, at least he could take over the family farm and milk the cows with his wrists.

Thankfully for my dad, frostbite was settling into Grandpa McVanBuck's fingers as well, prompting Grandpa to call the practice off due to the weather conditions before significant damage settled in, to either of them.

Now, when I was in my mid-teens, I would go work for the neighbour. This is where I could drum up a few bucks. Many of these jobs involved heavy manual labour like picking rocks and roots from the neighbour's field that was freshly cleared of its trees, as it was going to be turned into farmland.

The man, who I worked for, would tell me stories about his days back in the 1930s. Back in his day, a farm kid could skin a skunk in a mere twenty minutes for five bucks, and still be smiling with glee. Five bucks, back then, was a good wage; for even the wages of a full-grown man were less than five dollars per day. So for a kid, this was a fortune.

Nowadays, kids are considered to be tough when they have developed blisters on their fingertips from the excessive playing of video games. Sure, they didn't get the opportunity to freeze off all their fingers, and they've had to settle for cellphones, the internet, and text-messaging to be entertained. We kids, back in my day, had hard work to entertain us. There was no time to put an ounce of fat onto our bodies, for it was burned up as soon as it was off of our dinner plate and into our mouths.

We lived in Central Alberta, where there were plenty of rocks to pick on our dad's farmland. A rock-picking day consisted of my siblings (my two younger brothers, Calvin and Nedge, and my two older sisters, Daisy and Zoey) and I going out in Dad's fields when the soil was still dusty after tilling in the spring, and picking up, by hand, every single rock on that piece of dirt. We'd pick up anything bigger than an acorn. This only consisted of ten trillion rocks. These rocks would be thrown into the truck-box of the family's forest-green 4x4 pickup. Those days brought in true family unity.

Every so often, we would find a gem such as a piece of petrified wood (which I still have today), or we'd find a boulder that was too heavy to lift. One such boulder we found on my Uncle Casper's farm. The boulder turned out to be the size of a small house. This rock was concealed nicely by an inch of soil and wrecked havoc on the tilling equipment every year. One of the rules of rock-picking was (for no particular reason other than the pure pleasure of picking rocks), "You keep digging until that rock comes out." Then *Voila*, a giant rock – the size of a house – is found.

The real key to a successful rock-picking day was to stay hydrated by drinking plenty of water. My family all drank out of the same two-litre, re-used, clear soda bottle. A very important part for a successful day was that I had to make sure I got my drink from the water bottle in, before Nedge did. If I did not get to the water bottle first, I was destined to see part of Nedge's lunch floating around in there, like a chunk of cheddar cheese from his sandwich swimming around – looking like a goldfish in a fishbowl. *Blah.*

When I was unfortunate enough to come in after Nedge, I would be forced to drink from the bottle because I was so parched and dry. I made sure to give him plenty of big scowls and grumblings, as I moistened my parched mouth...sometimes even having to chew on the water a few times while I was drinking.

As I also learned, keeping my shirt on my back was key to preventing my back from looking like a cooked red lobster by the day's end. Once my back was the colour of a melted road pylon, there would be little hope of keeping my brothers from "patting" me on my back like I was their new-found pet lobster that needed a petting and saying things like, "Hot day there, Red, eh?" *Slap* "...those look like blisters forming there on your back." *Slap*

I would follow the brotherly slapping of my shoulders by giving a shrill, "Ow! Calvin!... Stop that, Nedge!" as I clamped my fingers like a pair of lobster claws onto one of Nedge's ears and onto Calvin's nose.

Then they would both squeal, "I give up! I give up!"

Now, as the rocks filled the back of the truck, one by one, the truck would begin to sink into the freshly-plowed black soil from the weight of the pile of rocks building up on the back of the truck as the pile went higher. The higher the pile got, the more of a challenge it was to keep the rocks from bouncing off the top of the other rocks that were in the truck-box already, especially if you were throwing the rocks from ten to twelve feet away. The whole time, the truck would be in low, first gear, slowly creeping along the ground. So throwing the rocks into the truck-box was not a frowned-upon event, we just needed to keep up to the moving truck.

No driver was required for steering the truck in the field. We would just put the truck into low, first gear, then jump out – leaving the driver's door open – and start picking rocks to save time. If the truck needed a little steering adjustment, then one of us would jump into the truck, correct the steering, and then jump back out to keep picking the rocks off the field.

If one of us kids stayed in the truck for too long, trying to sneak in a little rest while we were at the steering wheel, we would start to hear grumblings and complainings from the small army of other family members who were feeling that we were not doing our fair share of picking the stones. If someone was staying far too long in the truck's cab, we would make certain that Nedge would get his dose of water just before the lazy truck driver could, so that the lazy driver would be forced to chew down some water as punishment.

Once the large growing rocky mound in the truck-box grew to the point where the truck's sides began to bow out, it was time to take extra caution to make sure the rocks stayed in the box without rolling off the truck and back onto the field where they had originally been picked up from. Also, a fast-thrown rock could, hypothetically, skip off the top of the load and take out the back window of the pickup truck.

It was at this point, we needed to stay on our toes so we could dodge the odd zinger, as a rock would fly past our heads from time to time. Most of those zingers were unimportant ricochets, the size of an acorn. It was at this point of the filling of the truck to its maximum capacity, that Dad would start to talk. Dad was not much of a talker, but when far too many zingers were whizzing by his head, he would start to give us kids that "look."

"Hey, kids! Whatcha doing?! ...watch out for the zingers! That one there's almost got me!" he'd scold us.

Perhaps these higher fears of Dad's were due to his aging and the slowing down of his reflexes to be able to duck the incoming zingers – particularly, when the zingers were coming in from multiple directions all at the same time. His words, most certainly, helped to motivate us to keep the rocks inside the truck-box, so they wouldn't end up inside someone's ear. The fear of potentially pelting somebody can be highly motivating to stay vigilant, lest you should get an accidental, return ricochet.

It was shortly after one of these talking sprees of Dad's, that Dad bent over to pick up another rock from the ground. As Dad straightened up, Nedge threw a rock the size of a large baseball from twelve feet away. At that distance, Nedge was in danger of missing the truck altogether, so he really had to whiz a rock of that size to make it land on the back of the truck, much like a shot-putter at the Olympics. (I am sure my entire family would have been gold medalists for Canada with all the trillions of rocks we threw as shot-putter practice.)

It was a beautiful sight, as Nedge's world-class throw unfolded in front of our eyes. The rock was almost perfectly round and couldn't have weighed more than three pounds. The rock took a perfect skip off the top of the rock pile that was on the back of the truck. It was an amazing bounce – as the rock avoided the truck's window completely, missed the side mirror, and then beaned Dad's now-rising head. Dad had been bent over, picking up a stone from off the ground; and as he began to stand back up, Nedge's rock nailed him on his head.

Dad's hat flew up into the air, as his head took a wicked right jolt. Pulled along by the momentum of his sudden head twist, his body quickly followed, going into a wild, hard spin. His limp body then slumped down into the dusty rocky soil underneath him, that he had been standing on just micro seconds before.

Dad's landing would have been a little softer, if we had gotten around to picking up those rocks before he got beaned.

For a moment there, I wasn't sure if Dad's head was still connected to his body as the truck temporarily blocked my view of his head. He laid there, motionless, in the soil where his feet had once been.

There are certain times in life, where time stands still, and you are not quite sure what has just taken place in front of you in slow

motion. And so we all just stood there… just staring down at Dad, for what felt like five minutes.

This was the time before cellphones existed, so there was no one calling 911. And this was clearly before the time you would come to the aid of a fallen comrade - so giving some sort of first-aid attention to our dad, who had just been beaned by a massive meteorite zinger, was not part of our reflexive responses.

This was the time in history where you simply froze, stared, and blinked your eyes, while your mouth hung wide open.

What we were waiting for what?… I have no idea. Maybe our lack of action was from drinking too much back-washed water, or maybe it was from the heat that was now scorching our bodies. Maybe our shocked behaviour was because the truck was slowly driving away, revealing Dad's concealed, limp body that had been temporarily blocked from our view.

Dad was just laying beside the truck in a pile of black prairie dust. His rock, that he had picked up moments earlier, was still clutched in his twitching hand.

There were no sounds, other than the sound of the truck slowly rolling away with no driver. G*rrr…*

Finally, Calvin's voice broke the silence, "Mom, is he dead?"

Mom, who like the rest of us was just

staring, answered, "I-I don't know. His hand is still twitching."

Zoey then piped up, "I don't think Dad's paralyzed, because he hasn't peed his pants yet. I read once that peeing their pants means that they're paralyzed."

Zoey was always such a smart sister.

It's hard to be overly sympathetic when one is suffering from heat exhaustion, aching legs, and dry, chapped hands; but family is family, and we did what we knew we had to do – stand there and stare at Dad until he came to.

I didn't really think Nedge had killed him because Dad's head was clearly still on his shoulders.

Mom got the truck stopped before it drove too far down the field, then she tended to her helpless man, who was laying in a heap.

Now, when most people come to, after being knocked unconscious or come back from the brink of death, it is a slow and groggy recovery... but not with our dad. He came up, after about five minutes of silently laying there on the rocky soil. He popped up off the ground.

Then he just started staring at each one of us straight in the eyes, about an inch away, with such fright that it had the effect of some sort of truth serum upon us. We all pointed in unity at the offending culprit – Nedge.

Dad scolded Nedge about the importance of listening to his commands and about not chucking such large rocks so hard when the truck was so full before someone really got hurt.

Dad spouted, "What if a stone hit somebody in their eyeball? Ya could've broken my glasses, or worse... broke my false teeth. Don't ya knows, them false teeth costs me a fortune?"

Dad then picked up his red hat from off of the ground to cover the large skinned, bleeding goose egg that was now growing, like an unwanted guest, on the top of his balding head.

Walking over to the truck, he got a drink of water out of the two-litre bottle, all the while mumbling to himself. Then he paused for a moment, holding the water bottle in his one hand, while gazing down at the rock that he was, amazingly, still clutching in his other hand.

It was as if he was thinking, *Where did this rock come from?... why does the water have cheese floatin' around in it...?*

With a puzzled look on his face, Dad placed the rock in the box of the truck, and said out loud, "Where am I?... Whose am I?"

Chapter 6.

^ ^ ^

^ ^ ^

Your Coffee
Don't Taste Right

You may have already heard tell of my neighbour Mr. Brown - the natural born leader (pretender or otherwise), through the rumour mill. These rumours were, of course, started mostly by Mr. Brown's own two lips. By chance, you may have also stumbled into his scent trail, while out hunting down a big bull elk.

At first, you whisper to your hunting buddy

Max, "Hey... ,Max, do you smell that?"

Max takes a good deep inhale through his nostrils... *sniff.* "Yah," *sniff, sniff* "... it smells like the city dump. What's a garbage dump doing way out here in these beautiful pristine woods... miles from the city?"

Then we spot the bull elk that we've been looking for all morning. He is now only eight hundred yards up ahead of us. He is peacefully eating grass in a logged-out clearing in the woods, when he abruptly lifts his head. The bull elk then turns his full attention towards his upwind side, snorts, and shakes his head like an incredible evil has just invaded his nose. Then the bull makes a mad dash for the deep woods, heading away from whatever was upwind of him.

Moments later, several startled flocks of birds erupt from the treetops, flying overhead out of the woods, making a noisy racket before silence rules the forest once more.

But the silence is quickly broken by Max's voice, "There goes our only chance at that big bull elk!... What's the matter with all those crazy birds?!"

"That's what I was thinking!" I respond. "Bigfoot scared them up, I guess?"

Then without warning, herds of deer, elk, moose, black bear, and animals of every kind bolt across the little clearing where the bull elk had been standing just moments earlier.

All these critters, running at full speed, were fleeing for their very lives, terrorized by something deep in the woods.

This kind of terrorized running tells us, the hunters, that the animals are truly frightened by something that's stocking them, and they're running away. Maybe something like a really big grizzly bear, or a Bigfoot. It could also be an out-of-control forest fire that would make the wild animals behave in this unusual frightened manner.

Then a few minutes later, stumbling out of the woods into the little clearing, comes Mr. Brown with his rusted old shotgun.

"Oh, it's just Mr. Brown," Max fumes in annoyance.

I then say to Max, "So that's what they're so terribly afraid of... and I know it's not his rusty shotgun."

"It's his strange washing disorder of soapleafobia." grumbled Max, disappointed by the loss of the bull elk.

"Well, Max," I say. "That's what Mr Brown said his doctor called it when he was handing out this free information. You know he gave me this free information without me even having to ask him for it. I would say he's proud of his new-found soapleafobia disorder. Its a real attention grabber."

Now, if you end up in town - doing your weekly shopping at Eagle Firearms Hunting Store - and happen to run into morgue-like fumes lingering in the air, you will know that they are, indeed, Mr. Brown's odors. His distinctive odors hang about in the air, thicker than any secret wind passed in the tight confines of an elevator on its way to the twenty-first floor.

One day Mr. Brown came by my house, which is a mile down the road from his farm. He had a predicament that he had been putting up with for some time, and he needed it fixed. I was honored that the living relic, himself, would ask me for some advice; but sadly, the advice that Mr. Brown was seeking was not about proper human hygiene or how to run a wet soap bar over one's skin.

My wife Joy first spotted him through the kitchen window, as he came driving up our driveway in his old white pickup truck. Her heart sank, and her legs wobbled with fear.

Seeing the sudden change in my wife's demeanor, I figured, it could only mean one thing – it must be Mr. Brown pulling into our driveway.

"Peter... our neighbour Mr. Brown is here," Joy said, with a long drawn-out sigh.

Joy, then, with a crinkled-up nose, went over to the door to let him into our house. I could see that she wisely took in a big gulp of clean air just before she opened the door a slow, reluctant crack. The door then suddenly flashed open, by an outside force that shoved it wide open, almost knocking Joy off her feet in the process.

There stood Mr. Brown and his big wide

smile.

He shouted out at me, "Howdy, neighbor!...
I can't let you talk my ear off today, Peter. I
have things to do."

And he set himself down at our table.
Spotting food nearby, he began eating the
half-eaten baby cookie that our baby had
been contently sucking on, while seated in
her highchair.

I glanced over at Joy, for a moment, to see
if she had noticed Mr. Brown devouring the
slobber-covered baby cookie. Seeing her gag
reflex in full action, I gathered that she, in
fact, had seen him eat the cookie all down,
even to the very last, drool-laced, slimly
crumb.

After regaining her composure, Joy quickly
rescued our now-crying baby from her
highchair and went to put the baby down for
her nap in the crib.

As Joy left the room, I heard her mumbling
to herself, "I guess it was about her nap time
anyways."

With the baby now safely out of harm's way
– away from the cookie bandit and far enough
away from the toxic cloud of fumes that were
radiating off of Mr. Brown and invading our
little house – I turned my attention back to
Mr. Brown. The strong fumes were far more
potent today, then his usual, natural, high-
octane body odors.

He began talking before I could catch my
breath to ask him why he smelled so strongly

of gasoline. I assumed that he had been siphoning some gasoline at the auto wreckers for his pickup truck again, and then took a quick hosing-down in the gas to cheaply fumigate his body that had been overrun by an infestation of jumping flees.

Mr. Brown's voice broke into my ponderings. "You know, my hens – they should start laying eggs any day now, but they're just not layin' very well at all. No, indeed-y! In fact, these twenty hens haven't laid an egg for me in eight years, and I'm gettin' tired of waiting for them to start layin'. In fact, I'm a-figurin' it's due to some bad science and poor breedin' practices at the hatchery."

The any-day-now philosophy of Mr. Brown had obviously past the expiration date of his hens' inner working mechanisms by a good six years.

Returning from the baby's room, Joy proceeded to pour a cup of coffee for our guest. Then she set a loaf of freshly baked banana bread on the kitchen table and cut a thin slice from the loaf with the kitchen bread knife. Placing the slice of bread on a small saucer, she set it down on the table in front of Mr. Brown.

Taking a sip of coffee, he then reached over and grabbed the whole, remaining loaf of banana bread and proceeded to hack at it with his dirty, rusted pocketknife that he had fished out of his pocket. He looked like the legendary, lumberjack Paul Bunyan cutting down a forest with an uneven ax, as he hacked away at the banana bread.

He made thick, uneven slabs and chunks of the bread before stuffing the pieces into his mouth. He gobbled the bread down like some starved coyote.

Watching the crumbs of bread flying through the air, Joy and I were speechless - as we observed this display of true, inner hunger in full action.

Mr. Brown then asked, "You going to eat yer piece of bread there?" as he stared at the remaining, single slice of bread that Joy had originally cut from the loaf for him to eat.

Before I could answer him, his dirty fingertips were already dancing on the remaining slice of bread.

With a mixture of emotions, I responded, "Ah... you go ahead there... you look hungry, Mr. Brown." And my appetite vanished faster than the loaf of banana bread had.

Mr. Brown replied gleefully, his eyes wide with delight as the last slice entered his mouth. "Great!... I will!" *Gulp, gulp...* "yummy, but... I ain't hungry... just ate over at Jack's place down the road... yer food just tastes plum-good, real yummy." He continued, only pausing to lick the crumbs from his grubby fingers one by one. "So yer comin' over to take a look at my chickens, and see if'en they can be fixed?"

"Sure... why not?" I replied. "I know a little

about chickens. How about I come over tomorrow morning?"

I was fairly busy at the time, but getting out of the house to look at some stingy egg-laying hens couldn't hurt.

"Great... can I have this?" he jubilantly asked, as he snagged a second loaf of banana bread from the counter-top, where it had been cooling after coming out of the oven.

He was now happily gripping his new-found prize tightly, like a football he had just snagged for the win, in the last fading seconds of a football game.

I paused in thought a moment, as I began thinking to myself... *I should be nice - for that's the Canadian way. But to just take something into your hands off of one's counter... now that's a bit over the line! and that's not even mentioning his hands... only the finger tips are partly clean! This is a stretch... for even the nicest of Canadian hospitality.*

Sensing my hesitation, Mr. Brown then got a pitiful look on his face and looked at me, like a sad little kitten who just needed some love, as the grip of guilt tightened on my soul.

I replied, "Sure.... why not...? you may as well have it," as I clearly saw a couple of hungry flees joyfully jumping off Mr. Brown's shoulder and onto the loaf.

Flees and hand-grime on bread doesn't sit well in either mine or Joy's stomach, as it's an unique, acquired taste.

"Wait a moment, Mr. Brown," said Joy, chiming-in, "I have something real nice for you."

And she left the kitchen for a moment. She returned, carrying an extra tube of my armpit deodorant in her hand. Smiling broadly, she handed it to Mr. Brown.

"Now you use this real thick like, you hear," she carefully instructed, "and we have plenty more if you ever run out."

"Why, I thank ya, Ma'am. Sure smells yummy," he said, as he removed the cap from the deodorant and gave it a good sniff.

He then left our house, clutching the deodorant in his one hand and the loaf of banana bread tucked under his other arm, like a bank robber with his sack of loot. It would have only been death, itself, that could have separated him from his new-found prizes.

Once Mr. Brown was safely out of our yard, I took a good, deep breath of fresh air, which seemed to do little good to repair the damage done to my sense of smell.

Turning to Joy, I said, "The deodorant was a nice touch and a nudge in the right direction, alright; but it'll do little good to bring back my sense of smell."

She agreed, "No, it won't help with that. But Mr. Brown did look quite pleased when I gave it to him, especially when he took off the lid and gave that deodorant a big jolly sniff. And I really wouldn't have minded if he had used some on himself right there, on the spot, but some dreams just don't come true... no matter how hard I try."

The following morning, I drove down the road in my pickup truck and turned into Mr. Brown's farmyard. Once there, I got out of the truck and walked up the front porch steps to his house. Avoiding the gaping hole in the floor boards of the porch, right in front of the door, I gave the door a couple of good, solid raps... *knock, knock.*

"Come in, come in!" I heard Mr. Brown's voice call out, before letting myself into his small house.

Once inside, I saw him poke his head out of the kitchen, around the wall, as he gleefully chirped, "Come in! Come in... have yer-self a seat. I'll get us some coffee."

"Ah... no thanks," I replied, "I'm not that thirsty."

But he wouldn't hear otherwise. "No... no, I insist. I got 'nough money for the coffee... it comes in from China, you know. I'll just add less to yer cup."

I settled down into a kitchen chair and watched, as Mr. Brown contently set about making the coffee. I saw that he was mysteriously barefooted.

Then I noticed that he had a pair of boots and a pair of long, striped socks inside of his electric kitchen oven. I could see there was a story as to why he was drying out his boots and socks in the oven, in such a peculiar fashion; but I was here to look at some chickens, and was not going to poke my nose into the ins-and-outs of drying out one's wet clothing.

Carrying a pair of yellow coffee cups in his hands, he turned and set one of the cups down on the table in front of me.

"And here's a cup for you, good neighbor," he said, as he settled himself down into a chair, across the table from me.

I answered, "Why... thank you, I..." As I glanced down into the yellow cup, my mind stopped thinking in mid-thought. l saw the cup was three-fourths full; obviously, it was that way because I was not so thirsty as to be able to drink a full cup of coffee. But the partly-filled cup was not what made my mind go blank - it was the dark gray liquids inside the cup.

The pause in my words caused Mr. Brown to look at me intently. His soft-kitten eyes stared back at me, forcing me to put his coffee into my mouth to show my gratitude.

Willing a feeble smile, I took a small sip. It tasted as bad as it looked. It strangely had little to no taste of coffee in it, but an overwhelming taste of swamp water. Clenching my teeth together, I made the big brave swallow. *GULP*

"Oh boy," I choked out, "Is that some special kind of coffee...?"

I looked for an easy way out of having to

drink down the rest of the cup of coffee, then I spotted it. I had found my way out. I wasted no time and watered his poor cactus plant that was sitting on the floor just behind my chair by the window, with the liquids from my yellow cup. Thankfully, the plant was within an quick-arm's reach so I could dump out the cup of coffee lightening fast, and not get caught doing so. The cactus looked as if it had not been watered in years – maybe even decades.

I had managed to quickly sneak in the emptying of my cup, while Mr. Brown had momentarily turned his attention to inside the front of his shirt. He was inspecting it, looking for the stray flee that had become trapped in there. The flee was, apparently, making quite the fuss inside of his shirt, as it attempted to fight its way out.

Becoming frustrated, Mr. Brown started smacking at the front of his shirt, making a rhythm of *slaps* with his hands. Every smack of his hand upon his chest was followed by a loud, "Ooch, ouch, eech!" Then suddenly an intense flurry of smacks and scratches erupted. *Slap, slap*

"You little scoundrel! You ain't getting away that quickly!" which was followed by another volley of slaps. Then..."Ouch!" *Slap, slap* "Why you evil little beast..." escaped from his lips.

Interrupting Mr. Brown's slapping, I said, "Well, thanks for the coffee... maybe I should see about those chickens now." And I pushed my chair back from the table, as I stood up.

This coffee was sure leaving an odd, ringing taste in my mouth, and there was this crunchy chunk that was stuck between my teeth.

"Yes, yes! Yer a busy man, Peter," said Mr. Brown, snapping his head up with speedy haste now on his mind.

He retrieved his boots and socks out of the oven, pulling them out like a freshly baked cake.

"Oh, ah! That's a little warm!" he exclaimed, as he juggled his boots in the air for a few moments, giving them time to cool down before putting his feet into them.

Outside, we headed over to his hen house, as I picked the remains of the water beetle out of my teeth that had gotten stuck in there with my first mouthful of Mr. Brown's coffee. I'm pretty sure that it was a water beetle, but whatever kind of insect it was – it didn't taste any better than his coffee.

Walking in the direction of the barnyard, we passed a small muddy body of water, not far from the house. One of Mr. Brown's fat pigs happened to be sitting right in the middle of the puddle, cooling itself down in the water.

Then I noticed that there was a small path that led from the house down to the edge of this muddy body of water. I didn't dare to ask Mr. Brown where he was getting his drinking

water from, and I hoped my suspicions were wrong.

A moment later, Mr. Brown answered the internal wondering of my mind, when he yelled out, "Get outta my drinking water, you dumb pig! I gotta drink that. I'll deal with you later."

Then directing his conversation towards me, he continued, "Already put the pig away earlier, musta busted through the fence. Got my feet all wet and everything."

Then he paused a moment later, as we came up to the pigpen and found the gate standing wide open.

"Oh," he muttered, more to himself than to me. "Oh, silly me, I musta left the gate open."

We finally arrived at his chicken coop with Mr. Brown proclaiming, "There they are - my good laying hens."

Puzzled, I asked, "Mr. Brown, good hens?! You didn't mention having good hens! If these are your good hens, where are your bad hens – the ones that aren't laying?"

"Well... come with me, and I will show ya the roosters," he replied, a little out of breath after the walk.

"Roosters?" I quickly shot back. "I thought you said they were hens that didn't lay."

With a big smile on his face, Mr Brown busted out, "Roosters don't lay eggs, Peter. Thought you woulda known that much! Ha, ha."

I resisted the urge to wreck his little joke

that he found to be so funny by explaining to him that I was very much aware that hens are female chickens, and roosters are male chickens. Both, indeed, are chickens, but both don't have the ability to lay eggs.... but there was little point in adding more confusion to his already withering, 90-year-old mind.

He then dragged me over to an old wooden granary that he had converted into an makeshift chicken coop to house his roosters.

"It's these birds in there, good neighbor. They... umm, need to be dead... umm, and that's what yer here for. I-I-I don't like killin' my animal friends."

Apparently, in his ninety years as a farmer, Mr. Brown had never killed a single chicken on his farm, as he had a soft spot for his animals. All the domestic critters that had needed killing, had all been killed by Mr. Brown's pa, who had passed away years prior.

And any chickens, nowadays, that needed to be killed, where done-in by good neighbors, I suppose, I mused to myself. I could hear something coming from inside the granary that sounded like birds, alright. But there was a real-deep meanness in their cackles. As I listened to the sounds, I found their cackling to be extremely intimidating – without me even having to see them.

Undaunted, I said, "Well... let's have a look at them."

Mr. Brown then pulled out his pocketknife from his pocket and said, "Here, you can use this on them, once yer got a hold on them."

I hastily rejected this proposal, "No, that won't be necessary for now."

I didn't consider his dull, two-inch-bladed pocketknife to be an adequate tool for this particularly unpleasant job that had just been sprung upon me, only a moment earlier.

He looked at me with his sad little kitten eyes again, for rejecting the offer of his pocketknife.

Trying to soften the blow, I then added, "I'm just fussy about using my own tools, you see?"

"Well," he sighed, "since yer offer'en to do the job fer me, then ok." And he opened the door to the makeshift chicken coop.

Peering into the darkness inside, it took my eyes a couple of moments to adjust to the lack of light. The dingy building only let a small amount of light in, through the cracks between the planks on the walls and through the now-opened doorway. I could see the figures of what appeared to be large birds.

Wow! They're really quite large and ugly, I thought, with a sudden startle. These roosters looked to have been somehow cross-bred with bald-headed vultures. The cackles, these birds made, sounded like a bad violin player sawing away on the violin strings, while using one of these roosters for their bow – in a manner of speaking.

Inside the coop, these birds were sitting, perched up side-by-side on a long stick that spanned the 8-foot length of the building. This long stick was just above the height of my head.

As my curiosity honed in on the birds, I leaned forward, trying to get a better look at them in the poor lighting. I saw that most of them appeared to be missing large portions of their feathers. They were mostly black feathered, with a few red and purple feathers sprinkled here and there. At least, that went for the remaining feathers that had not been plucked and busted off, due to the apparent vicious fighting amongst themselves. These foul birds carried a real meanness about them, and they had a deranged look in their eyes that made me think twice about engaging with them in any meaningful way. They were staring back at me, at least the ones who still had their eyes intact.

I was cautiously making my way deeper into the building, as my eyes were still adjusting to the lack of light. As I moved in slowly through the doorway, Mr. Brown started to whisper something to me. But I wasn't fully able to hear what he was saying, for he was now mumbling very softly, which was not what he did normally in his speech.

Pausing, I asked him, "What did you say?... What are you mumbling about?"

He whispered something back to me that ended with a big *"shhhh!"*

I could hardly see Mr. Brown in the darkness of the wooden granary... and now, after another bumbling blur of whispered words, I could not even hear him.

With a great deal of annoyance in my voice, I finally yelled out, "Speak up, man! Quit the mumbling... I haven't heard a word you've said!"

Then it all happened so quickly, in a blur of confusion. All carnage broke loose at once, as the twenty twisted-in-the-mind cock roosters immediately descended straight down upon us, from their upper perch. Feet first, they dive-bombed us. Their nails and long spurs were coming in fast. But the "us" quickly turned into the "just me," as Mr. Brown had already abandoned me and was heading for the granary door.

As he gracefully dove headfirst out of the coop doorway, he reminded me of a seagull, diving for an old sandwich, laying discarded on the sand at the beach. For being ninety years old, Mr Brown had reflexes that could've given him a job as a professional baseball player diving for the stolen bases. For such an old man, he sure could still move.

I was a good six feet behind Mr. Brown, when those foul birds made their descent upon me from the heavens. At this point, there was no hope of me making my own survival dive to escape, even though it did cross my mind for a moment as things went

into slow motion.

So I decided, in the briefest of microseconds, to go into my full-offense mode. Fight or flight, they say, and I chose to stand up and fight like a man against these lunatic barbarians that were coming in at me from above.

I then fought for my life, as the swarm of angry, evil birds descended upon me - two or three roosters crashing into me at a time. They were emitting loud, scary shrieks as they descended upon me.

I was able to get in a couple of swats at them, as I tried redirecting them out of the air, away from me – before they stabbed me with their spurs. At least, that is what I thought I was doing; but their spurs, located on the back of their legs, were painfully overwhelming my redirection attempts.

Spurs, as you may already know, are a two-inch-long spear on the back of the roosters' legs, about an inch up from the bottom of their feet. They're kinda like an extra, misplaced toenail. The older the rooster gets, the longer and fatter these darts grow – until they are approximately as fat as a pencil and razor-sharp at the tip. When the roosters are in their fighting-mode, they fly with their feet forward and upwards; and those spurs are pointed directly at you, as the roosters attempt to use you like a pincushion.

Sensing that I was losing the battle, I then switched to my defensive posture, making one-handed swings at the roosters while using my other arm and hand to cover my eyeballs.

Their dirty, chicken-manure-covered spurs were so sharp, long, and deadly, that they sliced through my hands and body like butter. I felt like I was being stabbed repeatedly by a switchblade that had managed to exceed the filthiness of Mr. Brown's pocketknife, but not by much.

This stabbing caused me to burst out with the odd yipe and squeal. If the roosters had only given me a moment, I could have explained to them that I was not there to be their new daily dart board.

It was apparent, at this point, that simply going in there and grabbing the roosters by their legs or necks, then taking them out of the coop, chopping off their heads, and making them into soup was just not going to be all that easy.

After that first, overwhelming wave of flapping, squawking, sinister birds armed with spears on their feet, the roosters assembled themselves on the granary floor.

This massive flock of birds, taking flight in such tight quarters, had quickly stirred-up a massive dust storm of dried chicken manure, feed, and straw. This made it hard for me to breathe as my lungs filled with dust; and it became hard for my eyes to see, as tiny shrapnel was pelting my eyes from all sides. I blurted out a few more yipes and squeals.

The roosters must have been saying to each other, "Throw dust in his eyes, and then go in for the kill!"

It was apparent that these blood-thirsty gangbangers had a great deal of intelligence, and knew how to work together with their switchblade toenails. This was their turf, and they were going to fight for it... to the death.

Perhaps I should have been a little wiser, and not gone into their turf unarmed. At this point, I sorely regretted not taking up Mr. Brown's offer of his pocketknife.

After the first wave of violence, I was still standing and was sort of in one piece. That's when they made their secondary assault – from the ground upwards at my legs, feet, and crotch area. At this point, I decided to start making my way for the light - while I still had two eyeballs in my head, which those birds were particularly going after, using the dust storm to their advantage. I made my running retreat with a flock of twenty monstrous birds clinging onto my back with their claws and pinching beaks.

I could hear Mr. Brown yelling at me from the safety of the outside world. "Don't let them out... NO! ...don't let them out! They're gonna get ME-E-E...!" and I could see that he was attempting to close the door on me, while I was still inside of the coop.

I yelled back, "It's a little late for you to start speaking loud enough so that I can hear you... what are you doing, man?! Wait!...

you're not going to close that door on M-E-E-E...!"

It was now obvious to me that Mr. Brown had picked up an extreme phobia of his old beloved roosters. And it was a well-salted phobia, indeed, to have such a high level of fear within him – to leave his comrade behind to be preyed upon by his feathered friends.

This made me wonder afterwards, just how he was able to feed and water those things for those eight years, without having them needle his flesh each morning?

I was not going to let Mr. Brown close off my lifeline so easily, and I frantically burst through the now-closing door, using the top part of the entrance to shear the flock of roosters off the back of my neck. It was like wool being sheered off a sheep's back. I squeezed through the crack in the doorway as the door slammed shut behind me. There were only wings, feathers, feet, and a couple of rooster heads crammed in the cracks of the porous door, as they fought to kill us.

I sat there on the grass beside the coop, catching my breath and trying to clean the burning chicken manure out of my eyes. I stared down at my bleeding, scratched-up flesh and at the various puncture holes in my bare arms, through my bloodshot, irritated eyes and a bleeding eyebrow. I then looked over at Mr. Brown. He had a strangely odd smile on his face, as he looked back at me.

"So... do you think you can snatch'em when

they're not lookin', and then do'em in?" he then asked with a great deal of hope and anticipation of brighter days ahead, in his voice.

"No way," I replied. "I'd be a lunatic to go back in there a second time!

There was no way I would be able to go back in there and catch those roosters by their legs, without them attacking me first. Even if I, by chance, was able to nicely catch one, I would have his other nineteen wicked brothers defending him to the death.

Aloud, I continued, "There's only one way to put these evil creatures out of their misery. That's with my gun, shooting them down like wild turkeys."

By the size of them, the roosters were close to a wild turkey, only difference was the excessive meanness of these roosters.

And with that, Mr. Brown agreed, "It's a done deal, then."

Later that day, I returned to his yard in my truck along with my gun, a long-bladed knife, and the regular chicken-plucking equipment.

Mr. Brown was waiting for me and quickly announced, "Ok, you go and get'em. I'm leavin' for a spell, while you do what you gotta do."

And with that, he was gone. His truck had left the yard and the dust from the road was already settling back down, before I could tell him that he was more then welcome to help with dressing out the birds.

I then went back to the coop of terror and systematically removed those roosters one by one with my gun, until this species of evil bird was put into extinction, like their prehistoric relatives - the pterodactyls. I plucked these vultures and bagged them all up very nicely for Mr. Brown, and then sat on his front porch while I waited for his return.

An hour after I had finished dressing out the last bird, Mr. Brown returned.

"Well, here you go, Mr. Brown," I said, as I tried to hand him a couple of bags of fresh rooster meat.

He replied, "No thanks! I'm not hungry. You keep'em… they're yer wages for helpin' me out."

I persisted, "No, no… they are for you though."

He boomed back, "No, no! I insist you keep them!… but your wife's delicious scented butter that she gave me for my banana bread, now that's real delicious. Made my breath taste much better, too."

Puzzled, I slowly responded, "What butter…?"

"Gotta go, neighbour," Mr. Brown sputtered out, as he dashed into his house and his door quickly shut in my face.

I could hear him locking the door after himself from the inside. Apparently, the terror of his roosters was still following him, closer than his cloak of strong body odours – even after the roosters' recent demise.

Back at my home, I gave my Blue Heeler dog, named T-Bone, one of the twenty roosters I had dressed out.

I thought on Mr. Brown's last words – about the butter that Joy had given him – as I watched T-Bone happily chewing on the fresh rooster meat. The men's arm deodorant that Joy had given Mr. Brown was the only thing that came to my mind.

Chapter 7.

^ ^ ^

^ ^ ^ ^

Heat Wars

The warmth and heat of the hot sun is enjoyed – even relished by many holidayers on Canada's beautiful, lake-shore beaches. Sipping their ice-cold sodas and all decked out in their sunglasses, the plus 34-degree Celsius weather makes for a perfect day for the beach-goers.

When I was a teenager back on the farm, I would have the pleasure of enjoying the summer's heat from inside the roasting confines of a dusty, steel, grain bin.

Nedge, Calvin, and myself would be vocalizing our inner-most feelings on these fine hot days. "O boy, whatta good time we're gonna be havin' today, cleanin' out those grain bins of death.. oh... yay."

If one wasn't listening carefully, they might have missed the sarcasm in our voices.

Inside one of these very dusty, steel grain bins, the summer's heat would soar up to the plus 50-degree Celsius range. Even with the little man-hole door open, the heat stayed well-sealed in, like a hot oven – it would help to cook you like a pork roast, while you attempted to clean out the bin.

This entertaining, yearly event would be enjoyed by our dad, Elvis, as he looked in on us, from just outside the granary's small door. Dad was the boss, The-Man-in-Command, because he, for some odd reason, did not respect my self-imposed 3-Star General status that I had worked so hard to establish with my two younger brothers by using a few simple, mind-control games to encourage them to shovel the grain faster.

I said, "Did you know, Dad, I've moved up the ranks of command? I have a 3-Star General status now."

Dad only gave me a long, awkward silence while frowning.

I took that look as to mean that he must not be jealous of my rank increase, like my two brothers were.

There were times, as a 3-Star General, that I tried bringing the suggestion to The-Man-in-Command that the war on grain shoveling could be best served by The-Man-in-Command, himself. But Dad was just not that interested in my helpful suggestions, even when I tried pointing out an important fact to him.

"You know, Dad, if you were the one moving the mountain of grain inside the bin, you could stay nice and warm. You'd be getting plenty of exercise, as well," I said, while smiling extra big and fanning the air with my hands.

This only worked to draw a significant amount of fury from Dad's eyes along with gnashing words from the commanding drill-sergeant's teeth, while whole chunks of his lunch sprayed upon my face - making me feel like Dad was knocking my rank down to a boot-camp private.

There would be little point at this moment, to stop and explain my military ranking any further; for, as Dad so kindly pointed out, "Any 3-Star Generals hangin' around here, sure ain't gonna be eatin' any food this winter, if ya don't get yourself into that bin and start a-shoveling' those foxholes... pronto!"

He would send us foot soldiers into the front lines of the battlegrounds situated in the confines of the windless Sahara desert inside these grain bins. We, boys, would

then wiggle and worm our way into the open hole in the grain-bin door, head-first. This man-hole, in the door, was about two feet in diameter, just large enough for our bodies to squeeze through, to get inside the belly of the beast.

Our battle was to shovel the grain into the grain auger as quickly as humanly possible, without getting swallowed up in the auger ourselves. Standing on top of the pile of grain that was rapidly dwindling under our feet, we fought to keep our footing while still shoveling. The grain was being eaten-up from underneath the pile by the four-inch auger that led to the grain-mixer, sitting just outside the granary. As we shoveled, the barley grain would go up through the grain auger, and land in the grain-mixer. Once in the grain-mixer, the barley would be crushed into smaller crumbs for edible pig grain. Then other goodies would be added to the mixer – like minerals and soybean – this all came together to make the perfect chop for our hogs on the farm.

This pile of barley inside the granary looked very much like the sand-dunes of the Sahara. Sometimes, we would even see the skeletal remains of a pigeon or squirrel that hadn't managed to escape the heat and lack of moisture inside the bin after becoming trapped inside. These critters would be discovered, laying on the top surface of the grain. Many times, we boys felt sure that we would soon be joining these skeletal remains when we fell over from the extreme heat... but we were greater than soldiers, we were country kids... and so we pressed on.

Being armed with three aluminum grain shovels, which felt as if they were going to melt in our hands from the heat, and only a single two-liter bottle of water to share between the three of us to help quench our thirst inside the steel, inferno of dread; we shoveled as if our lives depended on it.

Dad insisted that he would have helped us if he could have been in two places at the same time; as he, of course, needed to watch the tractor's running engine, which powered the grain-mixer as it filled up with grain from the four-inch auger. And if the auger ever started to eat up one of us boys, he would be able to turn it off in time. But in our eyes, Dad sure did look mighty comfortable watching us cook like a bunch of baked potatoes wrapped in tinfoil and placed over a nicely roasting campfire.

The reason for us boys to be on the inside of the granary bins was that the bottoms of the bins were flat; and the grain, stuck in the corners and sides of the bins, could not be reached by the short auger. So it was our job to shovel the grain from the corners of the bin, into the auger. This was all to be done at a neck-breaking speed, to keep the auger from going dry of grain. If the auger did go dry, Dad would be reminding us of the food we'd be needing for the winter, and we had best shovel a little faster.

Secretly, my brothers and I figured that one of the reasons why Dad wanted us to get the job done so quickly, was so that he could stay entertained by our flying shovels digging into the golden grain – making him feel like he was making money. We boys, of course, would have been his slave crew, pounding away at his goldmine for the riches he would obtain.

Things got interesting once our shovels started to fly into this grain, which just so happened to be full of dust – a lot of dust. Our shoveling created a massive, hazy dust storm within the bin. This dust was in a single word, "evil". It created a significant amount of itching in our eyes, itching down our necks, and itching in every crack and crevice on our bodies. This dust, of course, was all un-pleasantly being washed down, over our bodies by the buckets of sweat that were pouring off of our heads, causing this enemy dust to stick to us like itchy mud. The only thing keeping that dust out of our lungs, noses, and mouths were the little white flimsy face masks. The face mask was our only line of defense against the swirling dust storm that lorded over us.

On hot days, this was a real balancing act – to keep that little white mask from getting soaking wet from all our sweat. Once it got wet, we were stuck - fighting to suck in some much-needed air into our lungs while working so hard. Air, for some reason, will not pass through the wet dust in a flimsy face mask – especially when that dust is layered an inch thick on a sweaty mask and has just become mud. Perhaps, the best that a person can do, once his mask is in this condition, is to turn it into a very nice piece of pottery.

Nedge had the brilliant idea of getting me to cut a hole in his muddy, wet mask so he could breathe again. But that was short-lived, as the air hole, indeed, gave him all the air that he needed to breathe, but it also gave him all the dust in the bin at once. He was like a vacuum cleaner sucking in all the dust.

I suggested to Nedge, that he shouldn't have inhaled quite so deeply while he was still in the bin and had such a big hole in his mask, as he was now gasping, gagging, and sneezing black mud out of his nose. With his lungs begging for cleaner air, Nedge made a mad scramble over to the hole in the bin door and stuck his head out.

After completing our mission, with this stint of labouring for room and board, Dad would turn the auger off. This would bring the conclusion (we thought) to our tour of duty in this desert of dust. We could then slither, one at a time, out of the hole in the bin door – like filthy, exhausted snakes – we'd crawl out onto the ground, wheezing and gasping for fresh air.

The-Man-in-Command, of course, would

snort, "Oh, quit all yar fake wheezin' and gaggin'. D'em masks ain't even completely black yet... look-y here, there's a large hole in yours?!? ...never mind that broken one. But you there, Peter. Look there. Sees the rubber band on the mask that went 'round your head, that's still white, ain't it...? Remember now, boys, you'll be eatin' good, come winter. Now get yarselves back in there."

Dad had such a way of looking at the whole picture – for eating was an important part of life and was a good incentive for teenagers, who needed the luxury of food to maintain an positive outlook on life, and we would worm our way back into the hole of dread.

Once we had shoveled the last shovelful of grain, we would begin yelling. "Hooray, we're done! We're done! Let's get out of this here bin!"

Our hopes would then be dashed as Dad, finished with emptying out the grinder mixer, would inform us, "Boys, I needs ya to do another load... no point ya's comin' out yet."

We would beg and plead in unity, "But..., Dad, we're all done!"

And Dad would reply, "Done? Cripes, we're a-doing three more loads today!"

At these words, we would faint and fall to the grain under our feet in exhaustion and despair.

Then he would brief us on the coming task through his slippery words, "Well, it's only one more load... after the next one. Then I'll give ya all a rest for five minutes... after that there, third load. And to think, if we made good time, we could even do another."

Perhaps this was a tactic to trick our young lungs into believing that they would have the opportunity to adjust to the real air again. But I was sure that the real reason was that this was one of Dad's military tactics – known today as mind games – to make the mind believe we were happy and content for just five minutes of clean air.

This trick of happiness to our brains was essential to regain the needed-mental strength to crawl back into the bowels of the grain bin through the hole, yet another time, and face the horror of shoveling the dusty hot grain for another hour to get the next five-minute treat of dust-free air.

As my mind drifted back to those hot summer days, it got me thinking. All the shoveling in those hot grain bins affected us oddly. It threw a trigger in Calvin's brain, in the wrong direction. Because just minutes after leaving the grain bins, once the last load was finished for the day, Calvin would suntan on the lawn – lying on his reclining beach chair in the hot sun – just frying there for another couple of hours. Calvin would do this, as if it was some sort of reward for himself – to turn his white skin into the brown colour of a roasted turkey.

The intense heat of the grain bins must've significantly altered all three of our boys' internal, thermal, adjuster switches. Because as for Nedge and I, our brains were not in much better shape than Calvin's.

For when winter arrived, Nedge and I were having an all-out, teenager war at night over the thermostat inside the house. In the basement, we each had our own, separate bedrooms; but we had to share one thermostat switch for the entire basement, which included our two rooms. Nedge loved having an extremely cold, downstairs bedroom. While I, on the other hand, liked the temperature in the basement to be what I called "warm" ...perhaps even a little bit on the warmer side of warm.

Because of the lack of a properly functioning, internal temperature switch inside of our human bodies, we needed to adjust the external temperature switch that was located on the basement wall. It was this little switch that gave us the power to bring our human bodies back into alignment and to the comfortable range within our own selves.

Things then came to a new low when Nedge began to turn the thermostat down to the plus 15-degree range. As soon as he wasn't looking, I would go over to the thermostat switch and crank it back up to a more reasonable position – closer to the plus 30-degree Celsius mark – to counter Nedge's dips into the frigid zone. Then a moment later, when Nedge figured that I wasn't watching, he'd turn that switch back down again.

As the heat war raged on, I began setting the thermostat up to new highs – heights in the range of plus 35-degrees Celsius. This lasted for only an hour before Nedge would wake up feeling too hot. He would then get out of bed, walk over to the thermostat, and turn it down to plus 2-degrees Celsius – almost completely turning off the basement thermostat. This would bring the heat down to new deep-freeze lows; and a hour later, I would wake up with my nose feeling a little frozen.

Then I decided that Nedge needed a more severe payback for these cold, unwelcome lows; and spending a scorching night in an African Safari heat-wave might fix his cold-loving ways, as the thermostat was flicked to the max temperature of plus 40-degrees.

And so this thermostat war came to a climax one evening, when Nedge and I kept running back and forth between our bedrooms and the thermostat, flicking the toggle switch in the opposite direction. As soon as I got the thermostat turned up, there he'd be, pushing it even lower than before. And in turn, a few moments later, I would be back over at the switch, cranking it back up.

As the war continued on, the time frames between the trips to the thermostat became shorter and shorter, as the thermostat was flicked from one extreme to the other, until literally, both Nedge's and my fingers were on the switch at the exact same moment. This created an all-out, finger tug-of-war for the control of the thermostat.

As we stood there, it became apparent that the other guy was not going to back down and leave the thermostat alone. After standing there for a good hour and a half in the middle of the night, as our fingers slowly turned numb from both of us squeezing the switch, we finally came to a mutual agreement. After much negotiating, we hacked out a deal. The switch would stay put at exactly the halfway mark, so that we both could go back to bed.

Later that winter, in the frozen month of February, the thermostat wars flared up again. Nedge and I were in the middle of one of our great skirmishes; and, of course, me being of the great military mind that I was – was not about to let those brains of mine go to waste.

I had noticed a small, little wire that lead to the thermostat. This little wire, I realized, could bring a permanent fix to our thermostat war and give me all the heat that I wanted, while also giving me the military victory.

So I went to the tool box, got the appropriate tool, and simply snipped the wire with the wire cutters. This little snip, of course, was done in a strategically concealed location, where it was not easily seen by the naked-eye.

Then I went to bed with a smile on my face and a great deal of satisfaction in my soul. I had outwitted Nedge's inferior intelligence with my 3-Star General status. I would now have a permanently warm environment in my bedroom. And knowing that Nedge would not be able to make it any colder – no matter how hard he tried – I went to sleep.

At about 1 a.m., I woke up bewildered. I was shivering cold, instead of baking hot. It, indeed, was freezing in the basement. Even the cold-tolerant Nedge, who loved being half-frozen, was awoken by the freezing conditions that seemed to be dropping significantly by the minute.

For some odd reason, there was no heat at all in the basement on this cold winter night. There must be a problem, and it needed to be fixed soon or we would all be putting on our winter mittens, toques, and snow pants for the remainder of the night.

At this point, Nedge, with his chattering teeth and blue lips, was trying to make the heat go up, for even he was really cold. Any adjustment he tried making to the thermostat failed to produce any heat or warmth for some mysterious reason.

"The furnace or something must've broken," Nedge said with a puzzled look on his face; and turning around, he headed up the stairs.

It was at this moment that I reckoned that my calculations had been a little bit "off".

Once you go headlong into battle, no matter how ill-fated the military strategy is, it's really hard to retreat. My plan had been to maintain the heat in its strength by simply snipping the wire, so that I could prevent Nedge – no matter how hard he tried – from lowering the temperature back down to a cooler zone.

Perhaps that wire will magically glue itself back together, I thought. For it was apparent that my calculations were very "off" and that this little wire was what relaid the message from the thermostat to the furnace to turn "on" the heat.

So by snipping the wire, all the functioning heat of the furnace was lost!

As I contemplating making an all-out surrender, Nedge reappeared, having retrieved Dad, Mom, and the entire family. They came down into the deep-freeze that was once their basement to fix our predicament.

But this turn of events – the appearance of my entire family – postponed my surrendering for a bit longer. Perhaps my lack of good judgment to surrender at this point, was due to shock and my violent shivering... maybe the cold had frozen my brain cells, slowing it into a slush-functioning mode.

Of course, everybody had their opinion of what was causing the problem.

"Did you try pushing this button?"

questioned Mom.

"Turn that knob," suggested Calvin.

"Hey, what does that lever do?" asked Nedge, flipping a lever.

Dad suddenly yelled out, "Quick! Turn that water off, ya knucklehead! Yer gettin' me all wet!"

This was the prime time for us to test all the knobs and switches down in the basement that we had been so itching to try out before, but hadn't had the courage to give it a wing.

Why... I even turned a knob or two, to just blend in with the crowd.

My oath of silence finally came to an end, when I noticed Dad's face turning from the freezing, blue-coloured look, to a fiery red. This is what educated people would call "being utterly frustrated". I knew I would have to surrender, but perhaps my family could be tricked into believing that the wire had magically cut itself, or that a squirrel had crawled up the wall and gnawed it off. This would most certainly explain the dead squirrel in the grain bin... maybe that dead pigeon had even pecked the wire off.

And so, while intently staring at the thermostat, I said as innocently as I could, trying to cast the blame elsewhere – to any other logical explanation, "Hmmm... What is this? A wire has been chewed off by a squirrel...!? I see, maybe a pigeon pecked it off... maybe even scratched it off with its pigeon claws?!"

Within a moment, everyone was huddled around me, staring at the suspected thermostat problem that my finger was heroically pointing at.

I was about to carry on with a few more detailed theories, when Dad exploded as he stared at the wire in astonishment. "What the... that ain't no squirrel... are ya kiddin' me? That's a clean cut, like it's been cuts with them wire cutters! Did ya say a pigeon?!... A PIGEON?!"

It was at this point, I felt the glares of my entire family on me, as scorn and a great deal of suspicion was being cast upon me as being the culprit of the cut wire. Perhaps the pigeon part had been a bit overboard, particularly, when I had added the extra part, where the pigeon had used its claws to scratch the wire apart. I guess I hadn't calculated just for how long that pigeon, laying in the grain bin, would've been dead.

One would have thought that my family would've seen me as the hero and saviour of the night; but who can blame them for not being able to truly think clearly when hypothermia was on the verge of permanently settling in, along with their violently chattering teeth?

So I chose to simply forgive them for not thanking me for finding the source of the lack-of-heat problem.

Dad went about repairing the mysteriously

cut wire. Shaking his head in a great deal of confusion and disgust at the logic of certain kin who dwelt in his house, he restored the heat to the needed, warmer level.

One by one, everybody eventually left the basement, shivering and shaking as they made their way back to their own warm beds. They shot big ugly scowls and disgusted glares at me, as they made their way past me and up the stairs.

As I stood there by the thermostat, I contemplated my heat-war ways. But with the temperature still a little on the chilly side, I cranked the thermostat up to maximum heat and crawled back into my bed. And by my calculations, it would be about one hour when the heat wave would strike Nedge, awakening him from his unnaturally human, frosty ways with a nice hot sweat.

Chapter 8.

Just Pull Nedge

Sunday morning was the day of the week for our family to wake up early, quickly feed the hogs, eat some breakfast, put on our best Sunday clothes, and then head to church. These best Sunday clothes, if all went according to our mom's plan, should not have holes in the shirts nor patches on the trousers. Grass-stained clothes were also not church presentable. We were frowned upon by Mom, if she caught us trying to slip past her unnoticed in the morning without our best clothes on for Sunday church. It was never made clear to me why she hated grass-stained pants so much, because my clean pants would always be dirty in forty-seven seconds after putting them on and leaving the house anyways.

If, by some miracle, our clothes were clean and holding together in one piece on a Sunday morning after one minute of wearing them, then there was a new record established for us filthy kids.

Dad would tell us kids. "You have to have goals in your life, kids! Not holes... I said goals, GOALS!"

Mom felt clean clothes with no holes in them for church should have been one of my dad's top goals, but it was his goal to do some fishing instead of patching his pants. Fishing was what also came to my mind first, because I liked fishing more than nice pants.

Once we were declared presentable, in a flash, the morning rush for the car would be on the way. Dad would be happily waiting in the front driver's seat of the car for us to come out of the house. He would be smoking his beloved tobacco cigarettes and coughing between puffs. Once we had all climbed into the car, then off we would go to the Dutch-Canadian Christian Church in town, twenty minutes away.

As a kid, I didn't really have a good logical understanding of the full purpose of a church, other than to see my loving grandparents, who also went to this magnificently large, cathedral-looking building on Sunday morning.

This church, understandably, leaned their teachings and indoctrinations on the dry, boring, long-winded side to see how much pain and suffering kids could endure before losing their minds. The church leaders obviously understood the importance of having a strong mind to be able to endure the heavy pressures of interrogations that break down the mind, just in case we kids were captured by the Americans, here in Canada.

Occasionally, there were good, exciting services, where we learned about the fear of God and His coming wrath on the wicked.

As an adult, after reading this fascinating church book - known as the Holy Bible - I found that it's full of adventure and intrigue. The Holy Bible is a book that has a total of sixty-six smaller books put together to make one bigger book. Some of the books are short letters. Some books can be very scary; and then there are chapters on the law that can be a bit repetitive in their stoning of wicked sinners until the many chucked stones made a mound. As a whole book, it is an excellent read and not quite what I remember hearing when I sat in the pew as a kid.

For some strange reason, these fascinating stories that are in the Bible were never read aloud in this church. Maybe they did not want to scare the little children with things like: seven-headed dragons, angels of God, and a talking donkey.

A talking donkey saying: "What have I done unto thee, that thou hast smitten me these three times? – would be shocking to a person and would out-right overwhelm any rational individual. I am sure that if this were to happen nowadays, the person riding the donkey would then fall off the donkey onto their head after fainting, because they just heard a donkey talking to them. But back in those days, talking donkeys were apparently common place.

I was just a kid who needed a little more adventure in church – a little bit more of the killing of giants, or the ripping of a lion in half with my bare hands.

Now, I do agree that fighting lions and giants can get a bit out-of-hand, like the time when my brother Nedge performed one of his own acts of valour. Nedge took it to the extreme by first jumping from the top of a fence, then onto the back of an unsuspecting, full-grown, two-hundred-pound pig. He then rode it wildly until he choked it into a sleep.

At times, a visiting preacher, who was just filling-in for the regular pastor, tended to be far more creative. The fill-in preacher would go hard core with the more frightening and violent books of the Bible, such as Revelation, Acts, Judges, and Joshua. These books contained great stories that would have me on the edge of my seat... stories like the gut-spearing of a fat king where the knife disappears into the king's belly, just like the circus act of a sword swallower – but faster; and then you have the story of a tent peg to the head of a peacefully sleeping man. There were also shipwrecks and the cutting off the heads of giants. There were also the stories about the disciples of Jesus being beaten with rods for doing the work of God, and the dreaded, seven-headed beast rising out of the sea.

Our eyes and ears were glued to the preacher with great intensity at these services. Mind you – when bedtime came, Mom was asked to leave the light on when she left our rooms, just to be sure that the seven-headed creature, with a tent peg in one hand and the head of a giant in the other, had not taken up residence under our beds.

The normal weekly service, on the other hand, tended to be a bit dryer on the side of adventure.

The preacher would say something like this, "T-h-e L-o-r-d said unto Moses, 'Blah, blah, blah,'" all slowly drawn out as if he was preaching in a southern church in Louisiana, and had forgotten that he was a Dutch-Canadian, who had never lived in Louisiana, or even in the United States for that matter.

Now, if the preacher could have come into the church with some live Louisiana alligators – that sure would have livened things up! A real burning bush or a venomous snake would have also been ample to keep me from being bored to death. I was a kid at the time; so what did I know about the entertainment industry?

The messages should really have been creative enough for a kid to avoid the strange feelings of being on the threshold of death. My penned-up energy was bursting out of my seams; my tie hung around me like a hang-man's noose, and I felt as if I was ready to die.

Mom had outlawed, in response to her kids' penned-up energy, sleeping in church; leg wiggling; and throwing paper airplanes from the church balcony.

Our paper-plane making had been outlawed for a long time, that was once perfected by myself and my sister Zoey. We found this out by making paper airplanes from the church news bulletins. It had been a great way to kill the loathe of time... until we could no-longer go undetected when the stirs became too great from the parishioners sitting beneath the church balcony, when the fleet of paper airplanes zoomed by.

Zoey and I had assumed, at first, that the parishioners would have appreciated our skills – not at just making paper airplanes, but also landing the airplanes on top of the ladies' hats and occasionally in the collection plate, as if they were aircraft carriers. If it hadn't been for the one measly, rogue plane

that poked an old lady in the eyeball, we could still be entertaining ourselves to this day.

Now the leg wiggling, I could understand that needed to be outlawed, as it kept all the men in our long bench awake from the intense vibrating of the bench. The prematurely awoken men would then give the leg-wigglers nasty glares, which were colder than the wooden church pews we sat on. The men's irritation was understandable – for it was the day of rest, and we were wrecking their rest.

A quick glance at Mom's angry red face would soon heat things up again, though, as she fixed more of her eye-bulging boogles upon us. Her eye bulges could have taken a rest on Sundays in our kids' opinion; but luck was not on our side, for the word "luck" was not allowed to be indulged in, on Sunday – the day of rest.

On the way home in the car, a strong and very scary preaching followed, as Mom preached on wrath and punishment from the Bible – if we kids did not smarten up, we would be going into the lake of fire. To me, this lake was not a nice hot springs in the wilds of the world.

One Sunday, we discovered the value of church unity. We five kids did not know at the time that working together, with all-ten wiggling legs working violently, in one accord, could awaken so many sleeping men at once. We had those legs really going, to the point that we were rattling the nearby walls.

This is when the Jones' kids, in the bench in front of us, joined in on our leg swinging with large happy smiles on their faces. At the time, their parents were not in their bench to stop them, as they were at the front of the church, singing in the church choir. And we McVanBuck kids had outright ignored our parents. With these kids' aiding-help, the paintings, hanging on the wall, started to sway and then one fell off the wall and crashed to the floor. We stopped the leg swinging then to look around; just in case it was someone else's fault.

When the painting crashed to the floor, it awoke the other three hundred sleeping souls in the church, who all turned to give us the death stare in a beautiful array of church unity. One would have thought that the paintings should have been more securely fastened to the walls; but it was an old church, and we kids figured that the wood in the walls must have been rotting.

Even one of the deacons had woken with a gasp when the painting hit the floor, and then hurriedly wiped the drool from his chin. One would have thought that a deacon had risen to the title of deacon because of his stamina and strength to make it through even the most driest of messages without falling asleep, much like a mountain climber who fights back all the adversities of climbing Mount Everest by a sheer-inner strength.

Sometimes there were other exciting moments, like when someone would be caught "making change." This evil deed of "making change" was made from the money already in the church collection plate. This practice of "making change" was understandable, yet was greatly frowned upon by the neighbour in the pew. "Making change" went something like this...

For example, a lady would put a ten-dollar bill into the plate. Then, magically, out of the plate would come a five-dollar bill, *voila*. This could only be accomplished, if a five-dollar bill had been put into the plate earlier by someone farther up the row. Also, this act could only be done if no one around you noticed. So this exchange was typically done, after giving a couple of quick glances over each shoulder to make sure no one was watching, before you would reach for the smaller bill.

My grandma once slapped the paw of a lady "making change" from a twenty-dollar bill, in exchange for a five-dollar bill.

My dear grandma had barked out, "How dare you steal from God's church!?"

She said this while at the same time, smacking the top of the offender's hand with her own hand, which made a very loud *SMACK*.

Grandma later told Mom, "Once it hits the

plate, it's God's money. Amen."

Well, up until then Mom was not aware of the infraction that she had been making. It was like some secret, unwritten, church code; and so this common practice of "making change" came to an end for my mom.

Each Sunday morning, each of us kids got one shiny quarter to put into the collection plate. This helped a great deal to kill the loathe of time. Those mere moments, as the plate made its rounds, were the highlights of the church service.

These were golden opportunities to test out the theories like – is the hand really quicker than the eye? And, how long could one hold onto the collection plate before being forcibly made to pass it onto the next sibling beside you before Mom's wrath started digging into your arm with long fingers?

We did not try anything if we sat beside Dad, or we knew that we would be dead. Mom, on the other hand, was like a dance partner with heavy feet. We kids simply needed to dance well enough to keep our toes from going underneath the heels of her shoes.

Another theory to test out would be - can you pass the collection plate over a brother's or a sister's hands without them noticing it? And also, can you keep them from trying to pull it from your hands, which were grasping it like a vice. This theory never worked out though, as I guess this was a much-needed highlight to the service for my siblings, as well.

The collection plate would make its weekly run. Starting at the front pew of the church, it would be passed from hand-to-hand as it made its way to the back of the church where our family would be sitting.

The back of the church was where Mom and Dad wanted us to be seated; this was for our quick get-away. At the time, this weekly stampede for the back doors of the church at the end of the service showed unity. The logical explanation of this church unity must have meant that we were fleeing the coming wrath of God, the moment the preacher spoke the last "a-men." With all four hundred and fifty people racing for the door all at once, this made the preparation for exiting the church extremely important. You had to keep an ear out for that last "amen"; then you bolted. It was just like the Bible story of Lot fleeing from the impending doom of brimstone and fire that rained down on the cities of Sodom and Gomorrah by the Lord of Heaven.

One particular Sunday, towards the end of the service after the singing and the preaching, the collection plate made its rounds, going up and down like a rolling wave through the long pews to our family. When the plate got to me, I figured that I needed to hold onto it for as long as possible before handing it to Nedge, who was sitting on the other side of me on the bench.

All cool like, Nedge grabbed the plate calmly with one sweaty hand. I guess, he figured this one-handed act looked a lot more cool than grabbing the plate that was loaded-down with twenty pounds of coins with both of his hands.

I don't blame him much for this miscalculation of the weight of the plate that week. This miscalculation was due to the fact that the girl in the pew next to us needed impressing. I, myself, had given up in failure on trying to impress that pretty girl after she stuck her tongue out at me for the ninth time. I was a little quicker at learning than my brother was.

Added to this, was the fact, that the collection plate had never before been that full of money. Normally, the five or six pieces of money would hardly add any weight at all to the plate. But this time, the rim of the plate could barely be seen, being loaded down with pennies, dimes, quarters, and paper bills. Plus, with all of those sweaty hands, all touching the edge of the plate must not have helped matters much, either.

Also, it seemed that "the wrath of God" message being delivered by the visiting preacher was having the desired effect on the congregation beyond the considerable amount of beads of sweat which were now pouring down the church members' faces.

This alone could have melted the January snowbanks outside. This moving message even got a very alert, wide-eyed deacon, who had sweat dripping down his lamb-chop sideburns to put a piece of money into the plate. I had thought that preachers and deacons were exempt from the practice of putting a nickel in the plate, but what does a kid know?

As the collection plate came to Nedge's, cool, one-handed grab, I could not let the plate get away so easily, for it was a heavily loaded plate and was a sight to be gazed upon for as long as possible. It was like looking at the inside of Fort Knox without getting a death stare from my mother's ever-watching eyes. At Nedge's grab at the sweat-covered edge of the heavy plate, the plate only slightly wobbled in my firm vice-gripped hands.

I had won round one, but only for a fading moment; for I sensed there was a set of eyes burning holes into my soul. Life is great. I like to live, so I began to loosen my vice-grip on the plate to spare my soul.

At this point, Nedge, from the other side of the plate was giving me an evil, angry look which said, "You are not going to win this today."

And with this look, Nedge jerked at the plate with both of his hands - now gripping it with two vices himself. He cast his impressing-of-girls aside for the moment, and put his full attention to the task at hand, which was to tear that plate away from my filthy hands. It was one of those life or death events, like ripping the vault door off of Fort Knox.

Myself, on the other hand, had determined my own life or death experience, which was to just give him the keys to the vault by making my hands completely reduce their vice-like grip to a wet-noodle grip.

Well, he was winning now. But this violent, two-handed, vice-grabbing, wrenching act made my brother jerk and pull with all of his might. And he, suddenly finding so very little resistance, got a very shocked look upon his face as the plate was now so quickly and generously jerked into his arms. And then it was making its way through the air and towards the floor. The combination of sweat, distractions, and the twenty pounds of coins all contributed to this unfortunate event.

Instinctively, without thinking, I kicked my leg out heroically at the plate, to try to save the day. What are loving brothers for, anyway? I could not let Nedge rot there, all alone. Maybe the plate would land on my foot as I kicked like a skilled gymnast and maybe everybody would gasp with amazement at my abilities?

Perhaps this would have worked if the plate had been completely empty, but it was not. That twenty pounds of weight on the thin saucer was all my foot could bear. The fast-falling plate that was filled to the brim would have been really heavy on my toe, even if my foot hadn't been in a violent, kicking motion. That plate was really heavy, and maybe the rim was made out of solid silver as well, because it really hurt my toe when the two made contact with each other.

I said out-loud with a howl, "OUCH! That hurt my toe!"

Then the coins and silver plate landed with a loud *Bang* on the hardwood floor, creating secondary echoes throughout the church. This was followed swiftly with a multitude of other sounds as *swishes, ker-plunks, pings, clunks, and rattles* filled the church. The plate rolled one way, as the coins all rolled in every other direction. The sound of rolling coins echoed into the neighbouring pews.

Then I whispered to Mom, "Why are you looking at me that way?... my sweet loving Mother?"

She was now giving me her death-stare that she must have acquired from the underworld. She was so terrifying to look at.

Who would have known that a collection plate could have caused such internal emotional injuries to a saintly individual, such as myself?

The plate, rolling on its edge, ran the entire length of the pew with a nice little wobble, even bouncing over feet that were in its pathway, for the plate was really moving along like a run-away wheel. Every single

coin in that plate had rolled out in every direction, making the entire length of the extremely large church building seem to be incredibly small.

There were no great "amen's" being blurted out at that moment, but we were hearing a great roar of whispers and disgusted sighs. It was a good thing that we were in the House of the Lord, where love and forgiveness are the corner stones of the church.

My family and I all slithered out of our seats onto the floor, just like melting ice cream. With our large cheeky grins of white teeth showing in our red faces, we tried to hide our embarrassment and guilt under the pew.

The following Sunday, someone else dropped the collection plate a few pews in front of where our family was seated. Then the week after, two more collection plates where dropped in the church in the same service – one was dropped in the main part of the church and the other from the balcony onto the congregation below. The coins rained down onto the parishioners like heavy hailstones, followed by a single bolt of silver lightning. It was becoming a pandemic, as "butter fingers" spread throughout the church like leprosy.

After the service, a deacon spoke with my dad, "Elvis, perhaps we should have some sort of rope or even a chain attached to the collection plate in the balcony," as the deacon rubbed the growing goose-egg on his bald head.

My dad replied, "I hears ya... I hears ya. Maybe some red baling twine would work, too; and you can tie the other end to your wrist."

That third "butter-finger" Sunday service was the last time I saw those silver collection plates. They were replaced with purple cloth sacks the following Sunday. A metal ring with three wooden handles attached, had been sewn into the mouth of each purple sack to hold it open.

And so ended the fast-spreading "butter finger" plague that had gripped our church for a month in history.

Chapter 9.

^ ^ ^ ^ ^

^ ^ ^ ^ ^ ^

The Miracle Man

I gave it all I had with one massive jerk upwards. I was attempting to lift the heavy wooden-framed bee box. The white bee box was two feet square and two feet high. This box that I was attempting to lift was currently full of honey and bees, and it was sticking to the top of the other hive box that was underneath of it. As my back went *SNAP*, my mind went blank.

A second later, my voice cried out with a

loud, "AOOOOOW," as pain and agony made an unwelcome appearance in the lower part of my back.

Obviously, my back was not in the mood to give me the hundred-and-ninety-eight percent of lifting power needed to budge this stubborn, sticky, honeybee box. My mind was willing and strong, but my back was feeble and weak.

I then paused a few moments to catch my breath, giving my mind time to think and allowing the pain to subside before giving that stubborn box one more large yank, in my attempt to loosen its grip on the heavy bee box underneath of it. These two hive boxes were firmly stuck together, clinging to each other like sixty-pound barnacles clasped onto the bottom of the hull of a ship. Shaking them apart was not going to be that easy.

I yelled at the boxes, "Loosen your grip, or else!" as I jerked and shook them again.

But to my great shock, the honey box did not come loose this time, either! It held fast, as if it was tightly super-glued to the bottom box by a good layer of thick honey and wax.

My back, on the other hand, did come completely loose with a deep powerful *SNAP-KER-POP!* This eerie sound rang out into the air from the small of my back, and it was soon followed by a lightning show that sent jolts up and down my spine and came out of the tips of every bone in my body. This let me know for a fact, that the law of pain is greater than the law of a forceful mind.

The third jerk at the box would have to wait for someone else with a stronger back, and a less forceful mind. In the meantime, the bees would need to fend for themselves for a spell, and my morning coffee could simply be drank black.

I then painfully made my way back to my house, still clothed in my white bee coveralls and wearing my bee-keeper's hat. Slowly hobbling on the heels of my boots, the bone-chilling shots of pain with each and every step were nearly unbearable.

After the slow, hour-long hobble back to the house, Joy met me at the door of our house with a surprised look upon her face.

"What's the matter with you?" she asked. "You still have your bee outfit on?!"

I stuttered out painfully, "M-my baaack, aawwww, is b-b-bad, awww, my back!"

Kindly, Joy then helped to remove my coveralls from my seizing-up body that was becoming as stiff as a pine plank, but shaped like the letter "Z".

"I'll give Dr. Zacherie, the chiropractor, a call and see if he can fit you in," Joy said, her voice filling with compassion.

A few minutes later, Joy returned to the living room, where I was already lying down on the floor on my back to relieve the lightning bolts of horrors and spasms that were blasting sporadically through my body.

"Bad news, Peter," Joy said. "Dr Zacherie

will not be in his office until Tuesday morning at 9:30."

"Tuesday, no-o-o-o way! Why me...?" I groaned, moaning in pain as feelings of utter despair overwhelmed me.

This meant that I would need to spend the next three days, over the long weekend, flat on my back before getting the needed repair by the chiropractor.

No fish will be caught this long sunny weekend at the lake... no dinosaur fossils will be found while exploring the back country, I thought glumly to myself.

As the minutes crept by, waiting for 9:30 Tuesday morning to arrive, I thought back to the days of my childhood – I was about twelve years old, and my dad had hurt his back.

That summer, Dad had been working at giving his farmyard a real good face-lift. He had tore down the old hip-roof barn to make room for the new hog barn. He had also dug some deep holes in the ground beside his new barn by using a shovel and a bucket tied to a rope.

The holes were most impressive. They went six feet straight down and were as broad as Dad's chest. These holes would serve as the holes to hold up the new light poles that would light up the barnyard at night, making the McVanBucks the envy of all Alberta.

When the hardware store had delivered the poles that Dad had ordered, Dad was excited.

The deliveryman yelled out the window of his truck, "Where do you want the poles, Mr. McVanBuck?"

"In this-here ground over here, of course!" came my dad's overjoyed reply as he waved to the truck driver to back the truck up closer to the edge of one of his new holes that he had so proudly dug.

Then with a healthy, "Whoa... whoa," from Dad, he motioned with his hands for the driver to stop.

The truck came to a stop, and the driver stepped down, out of the truck's cab. After giving his back a good stretching, he stood there, eyeing my brother Nedge and I up and down for a moment.

The driver was unshaven, with a three-day's growth on his face. His shirt was half-way unbuttoned, and he was showing off his very hairy chest. He had large cauliflower ears that were more than likely caused by years of wrestling as he attempted make the Canadian Olympic team. He then hiked his pants, which had wiggling down a bit while he was driving, back up over his belly.

Then giving a mean, half-hearted chuckle, "Ha... ha," he then proceed to spit a large mouthful of chewing tobacco out of his mouth.

I leapt back a foot, but I was a moment too late to avoid the loogie of thick brown tobacco slim that landed on the toes of my shoes.

"Stay on your toes, kids!" he smirked. "That stuff, it'll burn holes in your boots... ha, ha...ha."

I was twelve years old, and I knew better than that...this was just plain gross. As the tobacco-spitting trucker went over to talk to Dad, I found some long grass nearby that I used to wipe the tobacco juice from the top of my shoes.

Dad instructed the driver, "Ya can just shove that pole right into that there hole - right off the truck? I need's d'em other poles over there."

The driver retorted, "Nope. Can't put it in the hole. That ain't my job, and the poles are probably six hundred pounds each. But I'll tell you what I'll do for you, I'll roll them off the back of the truck for ya."

He then loosened the chains off of the poles that held them to the flatbed of the truck, and then gave one of the poles a kick that sent it rolling onto the ground.

As he was about to kick the next pole off of the truck, Dad cried out, "NO! NOT HERE! NOT HERE!"

But Dad's cry and the frantic waving of his arms came too late as the truck driver gave a fast kick to the last two poles, sending them rolling off the edge of the truck's flatbed.

In the next moment, the truck driver was back in his truck and was speeding out of the farmyard.

Dad stared down at the three poles laying

there on the ground.

Then he turned to Nedge and me and asked, "Now, what'em I gonna do to move them poles into the holes?"

Grumbling a few words under his breath, Dad then bent over and wrapped his arms around the end of one of the poles. He worked his hands underneath the pole until he could clasp his hands together, locking his fingers into place to ensure his firm grip.

Then heaving for all he was worth, he attempted to lift the six-hundred-pound power pole by himself, to get it upright in the new hole that he had dug.

Nedge spoke up. "Lift with your back, Dad," he encouraged. "Lift with your back, so you don't hurt your knees!"

Dad sang out, "I a-know's what's I'm a-doin'. Don't rush me, kid. Now, grab hold of the pole and help with the liftin'."

I soon joined into the effort, as we attempted to lift the thirty-foot long wooden pole upright and into the hole. Dad tightened his grip on the power pole, as he also tightened his grip on the cigarette dangling between his puckered lips, and together we gave the pole another might heave-ho. A slew of loud, hard, grunting sounds filled the air, before we all heard *CRACK!* It rang out so loud that I, at first, thought that the power pole had cracked in half.

A war cry of agony immediately followed, as Dad howled, "Awwwwwwawa!... me's back, me's back!"

I am not sure if the three of us had managed to lift the pole a single inch, but we sure had given it our all. The pain in Dad's back was so intense that he abandoned the pole lifting and headed for the house, as whimpers of sorrows escaped out of his mouth with every step he took.

As Dad closed the house door behind him after his painful walk, Nedge turned to me and said with a question in his voice, "At least he didn't hurt his knees...right?"

After a long pause, I replied, "Right you are, Nedge, right you are..."

Bob - The Water Witcher

A week had past since the pole lifting had been attempted, failing as quickly as it had begun. And Dad had not recovered much from his major back injury. He had been hobbling around, hunched so far over that one could have easily sat on his back, using it as a nifty stool. But he looked to be in a considerable amount of pain, which prevented anyone from doing so.

Going to see a chiropractor was not an option for him, for his own words were, "D'em chiropractors are quacks... a waste of my money."

Visiting a doctor, even with free Canadian health care was not an option either, for Dad would grumpily reply to those suggestions with, "Does me looks, like I'm a-needing my knees replaced?"

He had not been sleeping very well, and this had put him into this real foul mood. Seeing that his light poles were not getting put into the ground, only added to his displeasure.

The next thing on the farmyard's to-do-list of upgrades was to dig a new farm water well (which, thankfully, would not be dug by hand). The current well that was being used by the family farm was barely adequate for all the needs of our large household.

At the time, there was a government grant for Alberta farmers that would be given when a new water well was drilled. This $1,000 grant would be given to the farmer, if he hit water when digging a new well. This way, the farmer could get some of his money back. This incentive encouraged Dad to do all that he could to hit water and claim this grant money.

Excitedly, he informed Mom, "Becky, free money! It's free money."

Mom replied, "I see in the fine print on this paper that it will be paid out only if you hit water... is that right?"

Not willing to be detoured, Dad responded, "Yah... well... yes, it does, but I's gonna hit waters. I's a-hiring a real professional, water-finder guy, for a small fee of only one hundred bucks! Just think 'bout all that water you'll be having! I bet you'll even have enough water to fill the bathtub full of water. Just thinks, a bath with over an inch of water, like to the tub brim... and it won't even get muddy. Wow-wee!" and he giggled to himself.

The farm's water well would get quite silty if we used too much water from the well in a day. If we did happen to use it too much, we would be drinking what looked like a glassful of dark, gritty iced tea. And there weren't any white clothes left in the house, but we sure had plenty of brown shirts and some mighty fine-looking brown tablecloths.

Mom questioned, "You don't mean Bob? Like as in... Bob, the water witcher, do you?"

Dad came back with words that sounded very convincing to me, as he informed Mom, "Bob's got a guarantee that he'll find the water! That's as good as money's in the bank. Guaranteed, ya sees'."

Mom replied, "Well, I don't trust Bob or his water witching. What if he condors up some ghosts of the dead or maybe even some demons."

Impatiently, Dad snorted out, "There's no demons or ghosts in the water-witching business."

Then, after a long pause while Dad was deep in thought, he added softly just above the vibration of his thinking brain and just loud enough for me to hear, "...at least I don't a-thinks so, 'cause I sure don't like d'ems ghosts, them ghosts are scary."

When Bob the water witcher arrived at our

farmyard early the next morning, Nedge and I were ready, watching and waiting, pumped full of excitement at the thought of getting to meet a real witch. We kept our eyes fixed on him, as he stepped out of his rusty blue pickup truck. We carefully watched as Bob reached back into the cab of his truck to retrieve a two-and-a-half-foot long rod that was made out of solid copper. The rod's circumference was roughly the size of a Canadian quarter, and it had a large round hoop that went through a hole in the top of the rod at one end. This hoop ring on the end of the rod was about the size of a large grapefruit, and it made up the handle of the rod.

Nedge and I found Bob's rod to be most intriguing, for it didn't look like the classic witch's wand at all. To us, the rod looked like it would work just fine for stirring around in a big black witch's pot, but as for it being the tool for finding water... well, that had Nedge and I stumped, just as to how it would work.

And as for Bob, himself, he didn't look like he'd be a very good witch at all, either. With his plain blue-and-white striped railroad overalls, and a loose pair of wool pants pulled up to his waist over the bottom half of the striped overalls, he dressed just like all the other older farmers in the area. His hat was a green ball cap with a John Deere logo on the front of it. I thought the water witcher would, at least, have had a pointy black hat sitting on the top of his head and a few warts on his nose. Bob looked to be in his mid-seventies, and was not overweight by much.

Witcher Bob stared uncomfortably at Nedge and I for a minute or two, as we waited for Dad to make his way outside.

Since the pole-lifting incident, it took Dad a little extra time to get his boots on while trying to endure the sudden spears of pain that dug into his back at random increments. With his hunched-over back, Dad painfully made his way over to where Nedge and I stood beside Bob's truck.

As we patiently waited, Witcher Bob asked, "You boys prepared to be amazed today? I'm going to find a gusher of a well, with this here rod!"

Enthusiastically, I replied, "Yes, sir! You bet... but where's your black pointy hat?"

Bob gave me a puzzled look, raising one eyebrow, as he asked, "What do you mean... black pointy hat?"

Nedge then cut in with a pressing question of his own before Bob could properly answer my question. "Sir, what do the water ghosts look like?"

Bob responded by staring at us with shifty eyes and an odd look on his face, like he was having a strange, ghostly encounter of a spiritual kind at the present moment.

Just then, Dad arrived on the scene, excitedly announcing, "We're gonna find some water's today, alrighty. Just phoned

Tony… telling him to get his drillin' rig over here. He's already on his way to dig's me a water hole."

Bob then turned his attention to Dad, who was of much more importance to him than a couple of inquisitive kids, for it was Dad who would be paying the bill for his critical services and unique skills.

Now, while I still consider it rude of Bob to not answer Nedge's and my questions, I do cut Bob some slack, as I reckon that the reason why he was not dressed up in his real witch's getup was because he was undercover. Bob was trying to spare himself from being taken by the town's folks, and put to death by a lynching for practicing the evil arts of wicked witchery.

(Nowadays, water witchers have got a name change due to this confusion and are now call water dowsers.)

"Okey-dokey, Bob," Dad directed. "We's gonna give it a try over here's… in the yard first."

The three of us McVanBucks walked around the farmyard, following the water witcher, who was working hard at his craft. With the rod in his left hand, Bob held the rod stretched out in front of him, as he walked. The bottom of the copper rod hovered a inch or two above the ground.

Not too many minutes past before Bob the witcher abruptly stopped as he found the winning spot and yelled out, "Yup, this is going to be a sure gusher, Elvis."

His copper rod began twitching, before it started to gently sway back and forth.

Nedge's and my eyes became transfixed on the rod, as the sways got bigger and bigger with each swing as the rod passed over the point on the ground, where, apparently, we would find the water. This was amazing to Nedge and I – to see the water witcher working his magic in front of our very eyes. The witcher had found water with his copper stick!

Bob then quickly pulled out an old gold pocket watch from his pocket, and he began to time the sways of the rod.

After a few moments of suspenseful silence as we three held our breath, Bob then added, "Hmm…. fifty feet down there… yes… yes… I'ld say there's water there. At least twenty gallons a minute, I figure. Yep… maybe even thirty gallons a minute.

Filled with amazement, Nedge then inquired, "Sir, how do you know how much water is down there?"

Bob answered, "By my watch, of course! But the watch does seem to run a second or two behind, so there's a little bit of guess work in it all, I suppose."

Dad gasped with glee and shouted, "Great Ericka! We'ves found the water!"

And tears of joy filled Dad's eyes, as he did a little rain dance around the spot.

This was like striking oil for Dad, for the

water well that we were currently using, could only pump out about two gallons a minute on a good day. And after only ten minutes of pumping, the water would then turn to black silt. So this was a big deal to Dad – to get twenty gallons a minute would be a major increase.

Bob had no sooner finished bringing his rod back under control, when we saw that the big red drilling rig was pulling into the yard about four hundred yards away from the spot where we were standing.

A moment later, Dad instructed, "Run, Nedge, run! Get that rig over here's fast! Tell Tony that we'ves found the water, and he needs to chase it down for us!"

With that, Nedge ran off with a smile on his face that was as wide as the prairie sky!

Exuberant, Dad continued, "Boy, oh boy! That's somethin' alright... all that there waters! Wow! Twenty gallons a minute! No more needin' to share the bathwater, and no more drinkin' brown grit!"

Dad then pulled a beautiful, crisp hundred-dollar bill out of his pocket and handed it to Bob, who slurped it up and made it disappear in an instant, like a skilled magician.

And Dad declared, "Bob, the deals' a guarantee, and soon we'll all be dancin' under the water that will be a-floodin' out of the ground so fast it'll burst straight up into the air. Whatta sight that will be!"

In all of his excitement, Dad did not see

that his hundred-dollar bill had already vanished before he had finished speaking.

Tony arrived on the scene in his drilling rig, in all of it's mighty glory to the delight of all of us. Tony got out of the cab and followed Dad, as Dad ushered him over to the exact spot for the rig to begin drilling the new hole in the ground.

Dad directed Tony, "Drill her down to fifty feet, and we'll find the gusher. Woo-hoo!"

Tony then went about setting the twenty-foot-long pipe up vertically. This pipe had a six-inch circumference. Once the pipe was in place, Tony began drilling the pipe down into the ground.

Yelling out, over the noise of the rig and equipment, Tony announced, "...ten feet... twenty feet... forty feet... fifty feet!"

He then stopped drilling, and we all watched intently, but not a drop of water came out of the hole! I looked over at Dad, who was looking rather stunned, and his face had suddenly gone pale with the lack of seeing any water.

"What do ya want to do, Elvis?" Tony asked. "Do ya want me to keep drilling deeper?"

Dad shot a glance over at Bob, looking for the needed answer. But Bob was trying to avoid any eye contact with Dad, as he could tell that everyone was counting on him to have the answers and to save the day by finding the water.

Finally, Bob responded, "The water must be

deeper... it's my arthritis. It must be messing up the signal on the rod."

He then wiggled his fingers in the air to signify a sudden pain in his hands and wrists, and he looked at his hands with disgust for letting us all down.

With a bit more soberness in his words, Dad turned to Tony. "Keep a-drillin', Tony, til ya hits the water. We's needs the water. It's critical that we's find that water!"

Tony replied, "I have two hundred feet of pipe. We'll go down to two hundred feet, but I charge twelve-dollars a foot... and if we hit water, that's gonna be extra.

Sadly, after drilling the two hundred feet down, there was still not a drop of water to be found in the hole.

As Tony began pulling the pipe up out of the ground, he asked Dad, "Elvis, do ya want me to try and drill in another spot?"

Reluctantly, Dad replied, "Well... we needs the water very badly. We'll give another spot a try. We'll give her a try over in that there direction."

Then we were walking again, in search of a new spot. We were off like a pack of Blueheeler dogs, following the scent of the lost water well.

As we walked, Bob went on for quite a spell, talking as he explained to Dad that this was the first time in all of his water-witching years that he had ever come up with a dry well. And if it hadn't been for a sudden flare-up of arthritis in his left hand, he would have hit water for sure. He also didn't want Dad to forget that his pocket watch was running a little off and needed a tune up. Bob then ended his speech by promising Dad that the new spot would be better than the first, because he was going to be using his right hand this time, instead of his left.

Then Bob suddenly stopped, and we all froze behind him - holding our breath as one would when seeing a trophy bull moose, just before the rifle is fired.

After a moment, Bob yelled out, breaking the silence. "Right here, men. One hundred and fifty feet down, twenty gallons a minute!"

And his rod swung wildly over the new spot on the ground. The swings of the copper rod were a sight to behold, as it leapt, bobbed, and danced around in large erratic sways.

Tony then drove up to the new location, and surveyed the surrounding ground, looking for the right place to set up his rig on.

Quickly glancing around, he spoke, "Elvis, this spot's no good for drilling on."

Dad snorted in shock and inquired, "W-what's the matter with our new spot? There's waters down there's, and ya're gonna get it!"

Tony firmly answered, "No...no, can't drill here!" as he pointed to a small blue sign on a metal post twelve feet away that read, "Danger! High-Pressure Natural Gas Pipeline Underground! Call Before You Dig!"

Tony continued, "Your witcher found a

gusher alright, but it's not water that he's found! If I drill, I'll blow us all up and send the rig flying, sky high. It's best we find a different spot."

After reading the sign, Dad's face went red with embarrassment for making such a blunder, and for getting so caught up in the hunt for water that it slipped his mind that there was a gas pipeline there on his property.

Bob, on the other hand, looked as if he was going to be sick after hearing such a graffiti picture painted of our near-death. Bob's eyes shot from side-to-side, as he tried to kick-start his brain into thinking of a good excuse for this most recent gaffe.

As his brain clicked into gear, he said, "Aha, so this explains the wild swings that my rod was making. It was a pipeline... I misinterpreted it for an underground river! Yep, that sure can happen from time to time."

Bob, regaining his composure after this brush with death, continued, "The water's this way... I can feel it in the air!"

And he headed towards the cattle pasture.

Off we went, through the herd of beef cows, stepping in cowpies as we went, which is fine if you have rubber boots on – then it's no big deal. Bob, on the other hand, was wearing shoes. His shoes stopped the bottom-half of the cowpies just fine, but the top-half of the cowpies ran over the top edge and down into his shoes.

"Wow!" Bob exclaimed. "That cowpie was deeper then I first thought," as he sank up to his ankles in a fresh cowpie.

We then all walked, zig-zagging around in the pasture for quite some time.

I was walking behind the group, when I noticed that Dad had picked up a baler twine on his foot along the way.

A long, square-bale twine was now hooked over Dad's right boot and drug along on the ground behind him, as Dad walked. This twine basically consisted of a plastic rope that made a giant loop out of a twelve-foot long twine. These twines were normally discarded after they were used to hold the hay bales together so that the hay bales could easily be carried by the farmer on the back of his truck and then stored in a stack as the winter feed for the cows. Once the bales were fed to the cows, the twines would be removed and then be thrown into the trash. This lone twine now hanging around Dad's right foot, dragging behind him, must have gotten missed when feeding the cows that past winter.

As Dad walked, he became completely immersed in his conversation with Bob about life and how badly he needed to find this water. I couldn't really interrupt their ongoing conversation to alert Dad of the twine on his foot, because Dad needed water – not interruptions.

Now, seeing this twine dragging behind

Dad's foot, I felt a great deal of responsibility to help remove it from his foot and put it in the trash. This urge was like some sort of pent-up inner voice telling me to help my dad and save the day as soon as possible, before somebody would accidentally step on the twine and inadvertently hurt Dad's back even worse. For it was quite a sorry sight – to see Dad walking around, looking like some sort of king crab walking funnily across the ocean floor.

I decided that I could craftily get the twine off his foot without saying a word to him.

I started to watch the twine very carefully, looking for a way to get it off of him without him even knowing that it was on his foot in the first place. As Dad's right foot moved forward when he took a step, the twine seemed to be kicked beyond the toe of his boot by a good six inches.

With the right timing, I thought that I should be able to step on the twine, as it was dragged along the ground behind Dad. I should be able to hold it to the ground with my own boot to free my dad from this potential snare of adversity, before it grabbed hold of him like a snake, surprising his victim with a bite of unwanted pain and agony.

Keeping in step with my dad, after four or five steps, I had memorized the pattern of the twine dragging behind Dad's right foot. As his leg went forward, the twine would then momentarily be suspended in front of his foot

for a split second, as his left leg took a step. It would be at this key junction that I would need to move quickly to free him from this potential disaster.

At the exact moment that the twine was momentarily free, in front of Dad's right foot, I stomped with a good solid jump on the twine that laid on the ground behind Dad with both of my feet – to really make sure that the twine was not going anywhere and that it would easily unhook itself from Dad's foot! Feeling a great surge of self-satisfaction that I was succeeding at helping Dad out – without having to be asked or thanked, I stood firmly on the twine. My kindness went beyond the need of youthful recognition for doing a kind deed and having such thoughtfulness.

Within a breath of time, Dad would be freed from this little danger. And I intently stared at his right foot, looking for the exact moment when he would be released from the twine. But to my shock, as his left foot momentarily paused and his right foot began to move forward, I saw that his right foot was somehow still firmly snared by the twine. It was as if what I had been seeing all along was a master allusion cast upon my eyes by the witch named Bob!

And for me to believe that the twine had been freed from my Dad's foot at least half a dozen times earlier!?

There was a split moment, when I felt that

perhaps I could jump off the twine before Dad's foot came to the end of its noose. But it was too late. The time had come and gone. And now, I closed my eyes and gritted my teeth, waiting for the upcoming, jolting yank of the twine.

Just as I anticipated, Dad's foot came to the end of its noose. With a hard jerk, the twine was pulled halfway out from under my feet, making me to stumble a little before I could catch my balance and stand upright again. But then the yanking stop, as Dad suddenly found himself losing his own balance as the twine caught him by surprise, giving him a solid, motion-stopping jerk on his right foot. Finding his foot unmovable, Dad began to stumble, struggling to regain his balance.

Simultaneously, a large *CR-A-A-A-A-A-CK* rang out, like the sudden crack of a thunder bolt out of the heavens. The echo of the crack ricocheted, vibrating in the air around us a good three times, *CR-A-ACK, CRAck. Crack....* before dissipating. Immediately following, there came a mighty roar out of Dad's mouth.

"AAAWWW-WWWWAAA!" he cried out, sounding like a grizzly bear in a foul mood.

As Dad lurched, trying to catch his balance, his spine suddenly snapped back into its proper place. Dad stopped his lurching and stood up, straight as an arrow. And like myself, he was able to regain his balance and stay upright on his feet.

The whole group of us had stopped in shock at the outburst of horror noises that sang out! We all turned to look at Dad, who had now been miraculously healed from his hunched-over position and had been restored to a fully-upright, standing man!

Dad then turned slowly around.

I noticed an unappealing look on his face, that was nothing other than the face of a killer staring at me. I partly expected a look of gratitude from him... why, I even desired it. Gratitude is what anyone would expect to get from preforming such a great, miraculous miracle!

I was his first-born son, and I had now proven my worth to the world – that in fact, I did have a real talent in preforming miracles with pure lucky, supernatural powers.

As Dad's eyes turned dark shades of red mixed in with burning shades of wrath, he became fixated on me. I knew then that I needed to flee away from him quickly at this point, for he had adjusted, in record time, to his brand-new, healed back! I fled to spare my soul, as he chased hard after me, flailing his arms in rage! I ran as fast as I could for a short distance, and then I looked behind me to see if he was still chasing me. He was, and was even gaining on me!

I yelled out, "But, Dad, your back! This is a good thing! Look at your back, it's healed!" *Huff, puff, pant...* "Dad, it's a true miracle!" *Huff... wheeze... Huff... wheeze*

These odd growling noises were his only reply, *"GRAAAA…"*

When I looked back again, a half-mile later, Dad had stopped chasing me and was now making his way back to the drilling rig.

Bob, the witcher, was almost out of sight as he took his cue to do his water witching elsewhere, before Dad returned.

Dad, now free of pain and standing upright, went ahead and drilled a few more random well holes, which sadly all came up as dry wells. Sadder still, was that so did all of his financial savings when the driller's bill was paid.

But not all was a loss - for Dad's back was healed in memorable moment of time, and I didn't even charge him a dime for my services. I was a blossoming saint of unorthodox roots… at least in my own eyes.

Chapter 10.

Raging Grizzly Bear

Our baby came in the fall, some years back when I lived in Northern British Columbia, Canada. I was newly married to my wife Joy for about a year, and we had just brought home this new baby-boy from the hospital to join our McVanBuck family. This was my first-born child, and I had spent all night awake, pacing the hallways until he made his arrival.

I am a patient man, but seventeen hours to give birth?!

I said to Joy, "Can't you hurry it up a little bit, so that I can go park our car?" which just so happened to be still idling on the emergency ramp and was blocking the ambulance entrance doors of the hospital. I was hoping that nobody had needed an ambulance in the last seventeen hours, as I nervously looked at my watch again.

I said to the nurse, "Look at that knob. It's got to be the baby's nose trying to come through to get some air."

The nurse replied with a wicked glare, "That's your wife's tummy button, you idiot."

"I see that... now," I replied, with overpowering zeal for the now-coming child.

Eventually, the baby did arrive. And after we got back home, my wonderful mother-in-law was waiting in our house to help with the newborn baby. She was up-in-arms at us for being late. Joy explained to her that we had to first walk eighteen blocks to the car impound to pick up our car before driving home. Ambulance drivers are just not patient enough to wait seventeen hours until a baby arrives.

With my mother-in-law in the house, a tight space can appear to be even tighter quarters and in our small trailer home... well, it was hunting season and there was only one day left of hunting to fill my moose tag, so there was no point being claustrophobic.

When the baby's first diaper was needing a changing, I didn't want to offend my mother-in-law by taking away her job, so I made myself scarce and went looking for a hunting partner.

My mother-in-law nagged at me, "You need to, blah, blah, blah... diaper, blah, blah, blah, before hunting."

She, indeed, was right; I needed to make that phone call to Matt, my hunting buddy, before hunting. So with a phone call, Matt was over at my house within minutes, full of enthusiasm for the hunt, for he also had a moose tag needing to be filled that season.

His enthusiasm was then heightened even higher, to get going on the moose hunt, when he started smelling the new baby's ripe diaper. With the new pungent and highly-motivating odour filling the room, we both burst out of the house door, eager to get the hunt started.

Matt gasped as we fled the house for safer air, "Whew-wee, did you smell that?... that baby stank like a hog barn!"

I did agree with Matt that my baby's smell did make my eyes water, but this was my family's honour on the line, so I had to threaten to leave Matt in the woods overnight with Bigfoot, if he did not say nicer things.

Matt is a wise man, and he quickly changed his tone and said, "Oh boy, you sure do have a fine cute baby there, and he smelled like... like a cute little baby. Now, now, Bigfoot still gives me the shivers up my spine...but not your baby. "

"That's right, Matt," I said, "You wouldn't want me to leave you out in those backwoods overnight in Bigfoot territory."

We made our way down the back roads into the woods in my old red 4x4 pickup truck. We got out of the truck in a nice wooded area and proceeded to load our rifles. Walking down a narrow cut-line that ran north and south through the woods, our path made a "T" with a wide pipeline which ran east and west, parallel to the road we had driven on. About 100 yards into the woods, the pipeline could be found.

I had discovered this spot weeks earlier, and my goal was to walk along the pipeline that ran straight through the woods. You could see for a mile or more along the pipeline, and this gave us a good chance of spotting the monster bull moose – the one that I had been dreaming of shooting from the start of the hunting season. I could also use the moose meat to feed my now-growing family.

The gun that I carried was an almost-new .30-06 Winchester rifle that I had purchased from my good brother Nedge, earlier that summer.

Matt's gun was an old .303 British Lynnfield army rifle, a mark four, which made hamburger out of your shoulder when you shot the gun. This was due in part to the steel-butted stock plate. Matt's rifle was high on the cool factor, being an actual rifle that was used in World War II. But twenty-five percent of the time, it would unfortunately tear the brass shell cartridges in half after firing the bullet off, when using reloaded brass cartridges. This made the gun unreliable for a quick reload.

When Matt would fire his gun, it made him believe that he was the one being shot by its recoil. This made him a bit jumpy – being intimidated by that steel plate. The gun's recoil would surely find its mark – colliding with either Matt's collarbone or his shoulder socket.

Standing beside the pickup truck, I put five bullet shells into my gun's magazine. And then I led the way into the woods, along the narrow cut-line that made our path.

As we walked, Matt was loading his magazine when he said to me, "You know, if you ever want to shoot my rifle, you're more than welcome to. I know how much you like this rifle." Then he continued on, "It shoots six inches to the left and four inches low though."

"How can you hit anything with that thing then?" I asked inquisitively.

Confidently, he responded, "It's fine, if you just remember to shoot six inches to the right and four inches higher."

"You know," I suggested, "you could adjust the sight on the scope and fix that."

"I know," Matt said in a reasoning voice,

"but then I would be shooting six inches to the right and eight inches too high."

We had almost reached the pipeline, when I thought I spotted a branch moving. The gun came to my shoulder in a flash, as I peered through the scope. I saw nothing, but I did feel a foot step down hard on the heel of my boot. Matt bumped into my paused stance, as I stood still looking into my scope.

Matt's soft voice followed closely in my ear, "Sorry about your foot, eh... you see anything?"

Feeling his hot breath on my earlobe, I whispered back, after staring for several minutes through the scope at the wiggled branch, "Nope... nothing we're hunting for. It's probably just a bird or a beady-eyed squirrel...or maybe even one of those large Canadian mosquitoes." I lowered my gun from my shoulder to my waist, and readjusted my foot back into the bottom of my boot and added, "...if it was just a mosquito, it isn't even big enough to be legal, even if they were in season."

Mosquitoes in Northern British Columbia, Canada are a nice big size... don't get me wrong here, but if you are going to go for a trophy, well then you would need to go north of Winnipeg, Manitoba, Canada. That would be a dream hunt come true, but you would need a blood transfusion after the hunt, if you used yourself as live bait. If you let enough of the little mosquitoes feast on you

for a while, you can draw in a really big trophy mosquito. The key is, if you start to feel delirious and drained – lethargic would be the word – it would be best for you to get your shirt back on, and seek medical attention immediately for your now-needed blood transfusion.

Once you've bagged your trophy mosquito, you can use its leather to make all sorts of useful things... like a really nice mosquito purse or handbag for your wife. This will save your wife a pointless trip to the mall to get a new purse.

If you are looking for a more manly item, you can make a canteen with a built-in straw from the hide of the mosquito... this is super neat to show your hunting buddy. You will just want to make sure you clean it out real good, before drinking from your new canteen for the first time. You will need to rinse it, twice at least. If you don't rinse it out, you could very likely be drinking the blood of your hunting buddy, if he was used as the mosquito bait to draw in the trophy, in the first place.

Have your doubts of how big a mosquito can get? Well then, you need to look no further than science itself, for there is a variety of mosquito species that is called the zebra mosquito. Now, I have never personally seen a zebra mosquito or even a zebra before in the wild, as I have never been to Africa. I have only read about them in books, but I would have to think that zebras are at least, oh... 500 or 600 pounds. Of course, it's absurd to think that there is some 500-pound mosquito flying around out there; that would be frightening, *b-r-r-r.* But a 5-pounder, I would think is reasonable to assume, and a 50-pound bull mosquito works into my imagination, along with Bigfoot, Yeti's, and Giant Panda Bears. Mentioning Yeti's, Matt and I think they are just albino Sasquatches, but that's just a wild theory. You can read all of this in my soon-to-be released book, *How To Gut A Mosquito & Other Small Game Birds.*

So the hunt moved forward onto the pipeline as Matt and I looked up and down the cut-line for a monster trophy bull moose. I also kept an eye on the branch that I had seen move. It was in a thick patch of brush, where the leaves were still on the trees. It was hard to see very far into the thick woods in that spot, even though it was a mere ten feet away. At this point, we were going to split-up and go in opposite directions.

I spoke softly, "Which way do you want to go, Matt?"

To the right of us, there was a hill that limited our view until we crested the top of the hill. It was about fifty yards to the crest. To our left, there was over-grown brush, making the cut-line much narrower. It would be difficult to see a moose standing thirty yards away.

I was hoping that Matt would be a fool at this point, and ask me which way I would like to go. I would have said, "We don't have time to chatter, so why don't you take the left and I will go to the right." I knew that once you had crested the hill, the brush opened up and you could see for a mile or more. There was a good chance you might spot a big bull moose.

But to my chagrin, "I will go to the right," flowed from Matt's lips faster than the shells leaving a semi-automatic rifle when a sixty-inch bull moose is centered in the scope of the rifle during moose season.

And so "Plan B" was put into action.

"I will go with you to the top of that hill and take a quick look; then I will come back this way." I decided quickly.

He agreed because, well... I gave him no choice, and I was his ride home. We made our way to the top of the hill, side by side, at a brisk walk. It would have looked to an observer to be at a running pace with added enthusiasm on top, but that is Matt in a nutshell.

In a moment, we were on the top of the hill, peering at grass and trees. Matt was in high-gear and wanted to make tracks. We made an on-the-fly plan to split-up, to cover more hunting ground. The plan was that if one of us were to get lost in the woods, then we would shoot three shots in a row.

And if Matt shot a moose and thought that his shoulder had been accidentally shot by his own gun, due to the large recoil of his rifle, then he would need some assistance with the moose and some help picking his shoulder-blade up off of the ground. So with a half-made plan, known as "winging it," Matt was off.

All he would say is, "Ya, okay. Let's get going. Let's go."

Then off he went, taking a normal man's ten steps in three strides. I guess, I had been holding his pace back.

I turned around and started walking back in the direction we had just come from. As Matt left, I began looking for moose sign on the ground in front of me. I then took three or four steps before lifting my gaze. As soon as I did, I immediately saw a bear only forty yards away, in front of me.

The bear was standing on her hind legs at the cut-line intersection, where I had originally seen the large mosquito on the leaf. This is where we had been standing, just moments earlier. It was clear now what had made the branch move, and it was no large mosquito.

Don't get me wrong, Canadian mosquitoes are fairly intimidating in their own right, particularly in large flocks, but bears are on a much higher level of intimidation in the back country.

The mother bear was not alone; two small dark balls of fur stood next to her. I froze on the spot, hoping that she was half-blind with cataracts and perhaps did not see me standing there in the open, looking right at her. When I froze, she got angry; and the two cubs bolted away from her side into the woods. The mother bear got down off of her hind legs, and started towards me in bounds that made Matt's strides look like baby steps.

Unfortunately, she had seen me and must have understood my walking towards her as a threat. Even though I was now perfectly still, she had obviously seen my threatening gestures towards her family, before I froze. She grunted, "Woof, Woof," as she leapt through the tall fall grass.

She came fast and smooth straight towards us. Oddly, she made me think of a giant beaver, the way she ran towards me, being so low to the ground, as she cut her own path through the tall grass.

My rifle went to my shoulder as I tried to get her spotted in the scope of the gun, but I could not. The scope was set on high-power to see far away, and she was too close. At that moment, a chilling thought hit me, sending a shiver up my spine. I had no bullet in the chamber of my rifle, and I had a very angry sow grizzly bear now charging me, at a full, enraged run.

Something you should also know is that I am a left-handed shooter, and my gun is a right-handed, bolt-action rifle. This meant that I had to bring the gun down, off of my shoulder to put a bullet into the chamber. It

takes me a moment longer to load compared to a right-handed shooter, even with the added incentive of adrenaline-laced panic.

I got the lead in the chamber and figured the bear was making a false charge at me and would veer into the woods at any moment. This was my logical evaluation based upon the fact that I had startled her, and that she was with young cubs and would have felt that the cubs would be threatened.

At a mere twenty yards away, she was still running at me at full speed. I reckoned, I would yell at her, hoping that she would see this as a fine time to change her mind and make hasty retreat. I was moose hunting, not bear hunting.

I yelled out a firm, manly, "YO!"

But according to Matt's memory, it was more like a scared, girly howl, "Y-OOOO-O-WWOOLEDODL!"

This tactic did not have the speedy, desired effect that I was hoping for; the bear was now almost upon me, leaving me with few options. Running away was not an good option. For starters, she was running so fast and was so close that I would not have gotten far before she mauled me. The second reason was – I was standing between Matt and this charging bear. Meaning that if I were to escape by some miracle, Matt would have been next on this bear's menu. So I figured, I would only shoot at the last possible second, because reloading would be a problem if she was gnawing on my leg or something. I could not afford to miss that first shot from the hip.

At less than fifteen feet away, the bear was still charging towards me with great undaunting speed. I pulled the trigger, shooting from the hip. I could see fire tear through the gun barrel, as she turned slightly to the left to get around a small bush and onto the small mound of dirt that I stood upon, which had been made when the pipeline was originally laid into the ground.

Everything seemed to be in slow motion from the moment I first laid eyes on her. Because she had been shot at such close range, I could see high on her shoulder that the hair fanned out flat in the size of a small saucer as the bullet entered her.

She went right into a fast spin, turning around three or four times there on the spot. When she was done with her spinning, she leapt straight into the bush to my right. She then spun around in the woods, making quite a bit of racket as she attacked every shrub in her sight.

Thankfully, it was shrubs, and not Matt or me that she was attacking with such violent biting and clawing. In what I could only imagine was her wanting to find out where I had disappeared to, she then regained some of her composure and leapt across the wide pipeline in two bounds in the opposite direction, to my left side.

While she was doing her dance of madness,

I was busy ejecting the empty shell cartridge. I then put a loaded shell into the chamber with the bolt. I must have been quite transfixed – watching her terrified searching in slow-mo, because I proceeded to eject that loaded shell. And then, I put into the chamber another loaded shell, just in time to see two black eyes lock onto mine.

She, obviously, had found what had shot her. She ran out of the woods, straight at me again. I assumed she had recovered from being disoriented from the original wounding shot and her spinning. She was coming at me for revenge, to tackle me to the ground like a football linebacker on an opposing quarterback. Then things would, indeed, look bleak and my body would not look the same.

So I fired once more from the hip. And just before she would have hit me with her full force, the bullet hit her square in the chest. She piled up at my feet on the ground, only seven feet away from me. I reloaded and shot her once more, just to be sure that she was dead.

Just then another shot rang out from Matt's cannon, two inches from my ear, making me see stars. Better late than never, for Matt to come to my rescue. At this point, with four chunks of lead now pumped into her, the bear was well... dead.

Yet, Matt spoke. "I should give it another."

With a bit of shock in my voice and ringing in my ears, I said, "Ah..." before hearing

Matt's gun ring out another shot.

There was now silence in the air, as I went completely deaf for a spell. Complete silence.

The bear was still and did not stir, as I recovered from shell-shock. It was obvious to me by the size of the bear's head, paws, and giant claws that she was about a 600-pound grizzly.

Then the voice of an over-excited Matt yelled out, "Is it a black bear!?"

I lifted the bear's large paw with the barrel of the gun that was still smoking from the recent shots; this was undeniably a grizzly bear with her long, three-inch claws on her paws.

I replied, "This is no black bear."

Matt gasped in shock and asked, "Is it a grizzly?!" as his eyes dashed back and forth.

"Yes," I replied, still in a bit of shock, "it's no black bear, just a really black grizzly."

"I was not aware of any grizzlies being in these woods," Matt said, in a puzzled voice.

"Me neither," I answered.

"Man, you almost got yourself killed there!" Matt excitedly continued. "Just so you know, if she had gotten on top of you and started mauling you – I'd have been there for you, buddy. I'd have been shooting at her then also."

My brain began to think of that unwelcome scenario – of Matt shooting at the bear and hitting me in error. The chilling thought of Matt's gun being off came to my mind – to think of him having to say, "Oops! Sorry there, buddy, for shooting you in the leg. I forgot to shoot four inches higher and six inches to the right, when she was on top of you. I guess I got caught up in the moment with that adrenaline rush."

Then another ugly thought filled my head – what if he had only wounded the bear with his first shot and then had his rifle jam up because of a torn-in-half brass cartridge getting stuck and blocking the chamber from receiving another bullet. It would have then taken him several minutes to painstakingly pick out the broken cartridge with his pocketknife first before the gun chamber could receive a bullet that could save my life. He would have been saying to me, "Hang in there, buddy, for a few more minutes. I've almost got it out!"

We then made our way back to the pickup truck at almost a full-out run, with our heads darting glances over our shoulders behind us every few seconds to make sure that the bear's husband wasn't gaining on us, for he was out there in the woods somewhere.

Once we made it back to civilization, we told the fish and game warden, Warden Art, about our close, unfortunate encounter with the sow grizzly bear and her cubs.

We were drilled by Warden Art for every detail of the whole ordeal.

We then made our way back out to the woods to reenact what had happened. I showed Warden Art where I had been standing when I had started shooting. He could see the brass cartridges from my gun still laying scattered on the ground, seven yards away from where the dead bear was laying that verified the encounter was truthful.

As he climbed back into his pick-up truck, he said, "You know, I would have never let the bear get that close to me before shooting." And then he drove off.

We didn't get our moose that fall, but thankfully, he didn't fine us or take away our hunting licenses or our rifles, as some thought might happen. And even if he had done this, I would not have changed a thing, for our lives were on the line at that moment, and a quick decision needed to be made.

I heard later that the warden never was able to capture the cubs, and that he had skinned the bear out (for what reason I am not sure, perhaps for his office wall.)

The following spring, I heard news that a farmer in the area had seen a pair of grizzly cubs together without a mother nearby in his field for several days. This appeared to be those two cubs.

The Grizzly Bear that charged me.
August 30, 2000
"Kill or be killed."

Matt's hand on the grizzly's front paw.

A younger me on the left and my hunting partner on the right – Matthew Johnson.

Clean Adventure Humor
McVanBuck
Call of the Lighter
McVanBuck
Call of the Lighter
Peter N. Mast
#1
Peter N. Mast
Purchase
Book
On
Amazon
iTunes
Audible
McVanBuck
Call of the Lighter
Now On
Audio Book
Download
Today!

McVanBuck Call of the Lighter

- **How Men Really Think**
- **Thrilling Adventures**
- **High Energy**
- **Strong Family Book**
- **Honest Laughter**
- **Easy Reading**
- **On Audio / Audible**
- **Easy to find On Amazon**
- **Softcover Only $14.95**

McVanBuck Call of the Light is a full-length, softcover book, and it's jammed-packed full of great funny stories, based on true amazing events. This book will have you flipping pages deep into the night. These thrilling adventures are full of great humour. You'll find yourself overcome with fits of true laughter.

- You'll enjoy reading about the near-death brushes with massive fire balls that will make you gasp in shock.

About the Author

Peter Mast and his wife Joy live in rural Saskatchewan, Canada. They had seven wonderful children. Peter is currently working as an equipment operator and a truck driver. He is also working on the third McVanBuck book for this series.

Other Books by Peter N. Mast:

2019
McVanBuck Trophy Mosquito
Special Limited Edition
Adventure humour

2020
McVanBuck Call of the Lighter
Adventure humour

2020
Audio Book: **McVanBuck Call of the Lighter**
Adventure humour
Read By Martin Mast

2022
I Saw Jesus Christ His Face Was Full of Love
Christian testimony of several powerful spiritual encounters with the Lord Jesus Christ.

2022
And **McVanBuck Guns, Grizzlies, And Scares**
Adventure humour

You can stay up-to-date and enjoy other fun stuff at www.mcvanbuck.com